MY ANCESTORS WERE LONDONERS:

HOW CAN I FIND OUT MORE ABOUT THEM?

by Cliff Webb

SOCIETY OF GENEALOGISTS ENTERPRISES LTD

Published by
Society of Genealogists Enterprises Limited
14 Charterhouse Buildings, Goswell Road
London EC1M 7BA

First published, 1996
Second edition, 1997
Third edition, 1999
Fourth edition, 2002
Fifth edition, 2008
Reprinted, 2009
Sixth edition, 2010

© The Society of Genealogists Enterprises 2010.

ISBN: 978-1-903462-61-4

British Library Cataloguing in Publication Data
A CIP Catalogue record for this book is available from the British Library.

The Society of Genealogists Enterprises Limited is a wholly owned
subsidiary of the Society of Genealogists, a registered charity, no 233701.

About the Author
By profession a director of a Lloyd's broker, Cliff Webb has been deeply involved in family
history for well over 30 years, concentrating largely on London, Middlesex and Surrey
records. He is a Fellow of the Society of Genealogists, a Fellow of the Society of Antiquaries
and General Editor (Probate Series) of the British Record Society. Under his direction the
Society of Genealogists' National Index of Parish Registers series was brought to completion.
He has prepared a large number of other aids to genealogists and edited many transcripts and
indexes to records, of which the largest is a series of over 40 indexes to apprenticeship
records of City of London Livery Companies, also published by the Society.

Cover Image - Foreground: *West India Docks* by Augustus Pugin (architecture) and Thomas Rowlandson
(figures) from Rudolph Ackermann's *Microcosm of London* or *London in Miniature* (1808-11). This image
is in the public domain because its copyright has expired. Background: Survey map of London,
Westminster & Southwark 1677.

CONTENTS

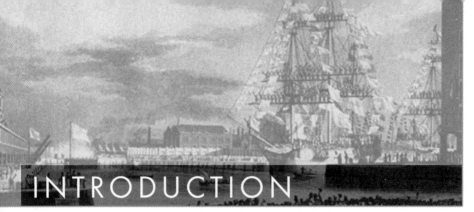

INTRODUCTION

The scope of this book and what is meant by London

One-sixth of the population of England and Wales live in the London area, and a high proportion of the population has always lived in London. Most genealogists therefore will have, sooner or later, to tackle the tracing of London ancestry.

Many, one suspects, give up, and seek easier lines - and it is difficult to blame them. Indeed, much London genealogy in reality consists of trying to get out of London as quickly as possible and tracing ancestry to some nice small country village, preferably with an excellent set of registers!

However, tracing London ancestors is not impossible, and relies on much the same techniques used elsewhere, however with different emphases. The purpose of this booklet is to review those techniques in the specific circumstances of London. It has been made enormously easier, however, by the development of internet resources. I know that there are many researchers who are unable or unwilling to use a computer. Unfortunately they are making an already hard task that much harder and for the purposes of this book I have had to assume that the reader is able and willing to use the internet or able to get someone to do that aspect of the research. Any book describing what is available on the web is bound to be out of date before it can be printed. Progress at making material available is rapid and while I have attempted not just to describe what can be accessed now, but what is known to be planned for the near future, there are sometimes pleasant surprises and any researcher should see what can be looked at digitally at the time. However, the other extreme has now been reached that some assume that if it is not on the internet, it does not exist.

Any genealogical study needs careful planning, reading and internet researching in the home in advance, before plunging into record offices, where many precious hours can be wasted by inadequate preparation. I make no apology therefore for recommending the perusing (if not purchasing) of a large number of books and pamphlets. It is perplexing that many people who accept that most skills and subjects cannot be learned without substantial study of written materials expect to be able to conduct genealogical research without ever reading a text on the subject! Many of the booklets recommended herein were originally compiled by me, simply because I could not find the information I required for my personal research in a straightforward way, or not in a cheap and convenient form, to assist the essential advance planning of research. Having created these items for my own use, my local family history society decided they would be worth publishing, and a cottage industry was born. West Surrey Family History Society publications are available from the Society of Genealogists, or directly from Mrs R. Cleaver, Beverly, 17 Lane End Drive, Knaphill, Woking, Surrey GU21 2QQ from whom a current price-list is obtainable (please enclose a stamped addressed envelope). The website is **http://www.wsfhs.org/Publications.htm**

This work concentrates on the period after 1600. The beginnings of many of the sources discussed pre-date 1600 but there is no discussion of sources which are only or predominantly useful before that date. The genealogist still finding himself in London yet able to trace back to 1600 has been both very skillful and very lucky, and pre-1600 genealogy is a major study in itself.

CHAPTER ONE
Administrative divisions

The administrative divisions of London are extremely complex, and the student of London has to have some idea of their nature or research may become confused. There were a large number of ancient parishes and also various entities such as 'liberties'. These were areas which for various reasons fell outside parochial and, indeed, diocesan control. Their inhabitants would worship and be registered at neighbouring churches. The parishes, together with the liberties, etc., have been grouped together at various times in larger units of administration.

Originally, parishes were grouped in 'hundreds'. Some early records are arranged by hundred, mainly records of central taxation, such as lay subsidies. The hundred is shown for each parish in the Greater London area in appendix 2. City of London parishes were grouped in wards, for which see below.

The most important grouping for nineteenth century research is the registration district. This was the area which is used in the Registrar General's indexes of births, marriages and deaths, and also in arranging the census returns. Registration districts are discussed further in the section on the Registrar-General's records.

Another cause of confusion is that the word 'parish' has been used to mean two different areas in English administrative history: ecclesiastical parishes and civil parishes. The ecclesiastical parish is normally the one with which genealogists are concerned, except when using census returns which are arranged by civil parish. It is the area under the ecclesiastical authority of an incumbent with a church at its centre (spiritually if not geographically). However parishes were used as the basic unit of secular government too, and there came about the concept of the civil parish, which could be, and increasingly was, separate in area from the ecclesiastical parish. For example, some ecclesiastical parishes such as St Andrew Holborn, St Botolph Aldgate and St Sepulchre straddled the boundary of the 'City of London' as described below. The parts within and without the City, in some cases known as 'Below the Bars' and 'Above the Bars' respectively, are usually differentiated as, for example, St Andrew Holborn, London, and St Andrew Holborn, Middlesex. This is because they formed two different civil parishes, and therefore had two different sets of civil parish records, but only have one series of parish registers and other ecclesiastical records. St Giles Cripplegate originally had a large part beyond the walls, too. In 1733, this was detached and became the new parish of St Luke Old Street. Pre-1837 changes of this sort north of the Thames will be found detailed in the National Index of Parish Registers volume for London and Middlesex (Society of Genealogists, 2nd ed., 2002).

The area of London has steadily grown from the medieval core of the City ('the square mile') to the vast, sprawling and rather ill-defined megapolis of today. The original City consisted of some hundred-odd parishes, mainly very small in area, encompassed by the old (originally Roman) City walls. This area had (and has) its own separate administration under the Corporation of London and the Common Council, an independence which is reflected in archives and their location. A mile or so to the west of the City was another early centre of population, Westminster. Westminster, too, ranked as a city in its own right, based on Westminster Abbey and the Houses of Parliament. The City of Westminster was the administrative capital of England, just as the City of London was the commercial capital.

The City of London itself was divided into 26 wards. Wards contained between one and nine parishes and are the basis of City administration. A few name-lists are arranged by ward, but in general wards have not themselves produced records of genealogical interest. A guide to the City wards, keyed to streets and parishes has been produced by West Surrey Family History Society[1].

Already, in the seventeenth century, there was a growth of population outside the two cities of London and Westminster. The corridor of open land between them filled rapidly; Southwark on the south side of the Thames at the other end of

London Bridge from the City of London was growing, and the network of villages surrounding London such as Stepney in the east, Hackney and Islington to the north and Kensington to the west were becoming richer and more populous, largely because of their proximity to London. A series of historic atlases has been produced which is extremely useful in showing this growth of the urbanised area and also in identifying places[2].

The area surrounding the City of London on the north bank of the Thames is part of the ancient county of Middlesex, while that on the south bank is part of the ancient county of Surrey. Growth continued unabated throughout the seventeenth, eighteenth and nineteenth centuries. Suburban development in the east continued over the River Lea into the ancient County of Essex, and south of the Thames into areas such as Greenwich which were part of the ancient county of Kent.

Until the 1830s, most local governmental activity was at the parish level. With the vast populations of most parishes, a select group of inhabitants, usually called the 'Select Vestry' assumed control and ran the parish affairs through a small number of officials, mostly unpaid and elected annually. Service in these positions was often resented and resisted, as it could be extremely time-consuming. In 1834 with the reform of the Poor Law, in most places parishes were grouped into areas called Poor Law Unions and boards of Poor Law Guardians were appointed. Many London parishes were large enough to have their own Boards of Guardians and constituted a single parish union. An inexpensive and convenient list of London Poor Law Unions and their records is available[3]. In 1855 the Metropolitan Board of Works was created with responsibility for sanitary matters over an area which became known as the 'Metropolis'.

The old system was gradually seen to be breaking down through the middle of the nineteenth century. It was decided that a strategic local government authority was needed for London and in 1889 the County of London was formed. The City of London retained its own administration, but in 1899 the rest of the 'Metropolis' was organised into 'Metropolitan Boroughs'. Some of the Boroughs comprised a single ancient parish, some contained more than one. There follows a list of the Boroughs. The ancient parishes contained within a Borough are given where there were more than one:

BATTERSEA; BERMONDSEY (containing Bermondsey, Rotherhithe and the Southwark parishes of St John Horsleydown, St Olave and St Thomas); BETHNAL GREEN; CAMBERWELL; CHELSEA; DEPTFORD (containing Deptford St Paul, Deptford St Nicholas being in the Metropolitan Borough of Greenwich); FINSBURY (containing Charterhouse, Glasshouse Yard Liberty, St James Clerkenwell, St John

Clerkenwell, St Luke Old Street and St Sepulchre, Middlesex); FULHAM; GREENWICH (containing Charlton, Deptford St Nicholas and Greenwich); HACKNEY; HAMMERSMITH; HAMPSTEAD; HOLBORN (containing St Andrew Holborn, the Inns of Court and Chancery, the Liberty of Saffron Hill, Ely Rents and Ely Place, St George Bloomsbury, St George the Martyr Holborn and St Giles in the Fields); ISLINGTON; KENSINGTON; LAMBETH; LEWISHAM (containing Deptford St Paul, Lee and Lewisham); PADDINGTON; POPLAR (containing Bromley by Bow, Poplar and Stratford le Bow); ST MARYLEBONE; ST PANCRAS; SHOREDITCH; SOUTHWARK (containing Newington and the Southwark parishes of Christ Church, St George and St Saviour); STEPNEY (containing Limehouse, Norton Folgate, Old Artillery Ground, St Botolph Aldgate (Middlesex), St George in the East, Shadwell, Spitalfields, Stepney, the Tower of London, Wapping and Whitechapel); STOKE NEWINGTON; WANDSWORTH (containing Clapham, Putney, Streatham, Tooting Graveney and Wandsworth); WESTMINSTER (containing the Liberty of the Rolls, St Anne Soho, St Clement Dane, St George Hanover Square, St James Westminster; St John Westminster, St Margaret Westminster, St Martin in the Fields, St Mary le Strand, St Paul Covent Garden and the Savoy Precinct); WOOLWICH (containing Eltham, Plumstead and Woolwich).

The Metropolitan boroughs of Battersea, Bermondsey, Camberwell, Lambeth, Southwark and Wandsworth were created from parishes in the ancient county of Surrey; the boroughs of Deptford, Greenwich, Lewisham and Woolwich from the ancient county of Kent; and the other boroughs from the ancient county of Middlesex.

London is for most purposes treated here as the area covered by these metropolitan boroughs which, with minor adjustments to the borders, remained the municipal administrative area until 1965. In that year there was a substantial change in municipal boundaries. There had continued throughout the twentieth century to be a growth in the urbanised area of London. Attempts to control this growth had and have been made, principally by designating a roughly doughnut-shaped area surrounding the built-up area as 'Green Belt' and not available to development. The principal result was for development to continue but beyond the bounds of the Green Belt. A modern-day researcher therefore may well consider as part of London an area which was not so considered until 1965 or even beyond that.

In 1965, the old London County Council was abolished and a new Greater London Council established. Almost all that part of Middlesex not made into metropolitan boroughs in 1899 was now incorporated, as were large parts of Surrey and Essex, and smaller segments of Hertfordshire and Kent. From the point of view of the researcher the most important result of this reorganisation was the amalgamation of archive services which most of the old boroughs had established. All but one (Havering) of the new Greater London boroughs established archive services and these continue, as do the Greater London boroughs themselves, despite the subsequent abolition of the Greater London Council as an overall strategic body. The record offices established by these archive services are too little known and contain much original material of use to the researcher.

There can be considerable confusion when the same name was used for a metropolitan borough and a later Greater London borough, covering different areas. For example, the old City of Westminster was a metropolitan borough, but the London Borough of Westminster includes areas such as Paddington and St Marylebone, not in the City of Westminster.

CHAPTER TWO
London family history societies

Local family history societies have divided up the London area. They cover the following metropolitan boroughs and Greater London boroughs:

East of London Family History Society:
Metropolitan boroughs: Bethnal Green; Hackney; Poplar; Shoreditch; Stepney; Stoke Newington.
Greater London boroughs: Barking; Hackney; Havering; Newham; Redbridge; Tower Hamlets.

East Surrey Family History Society:
Metropolitan boroughs: Battersea; Bermondsey; Camberwell; Lambeth; Southwark; Wandsworth.
Greater London boroughs: Croydon; Kingston; Lambeth; Merton; Richmond (part); Southwark; Sutton; Wandsworth.

Hillingdon Family History Society:
Greater London borough: Hillingdon.

London Westminster and North Middlesex Family History Society:
City of London.
Metropolitan boroughs: Finsbury; Hampstead; Holborn; Islington; St Marylebone; St Pancras; Westminster.

Greater London boroughs: Barnet; Brent; Camden; Enfield; Haringey; Harrow; Hillingdon (part); Islington; Westminster.

North West Kent Family History Society:
Metropolitan boroughs: Deptford; Greenwich; Lewisham; Woolwich.
Greater London boroughs: Bexley; Bromley; Greenwich; Lewisham.

Waltham Forest Family History Society:
Greater London borough: Waltham Forest.

West Middlesex Family History Society:
Metropolitan boroughs: Chelsea; Fulham; Hammersmith; Kensington; Paddington.
Greater London boroughs: Ealing; Hammersmith; Hillingdon (part); Hounslow; Kensington and Chelsea; Richmond (part).
Westminster and Central Middlesex Family History Society has amalgamated with the City of London and North Middlesex Family History Society to form London Westminster and North Middlesex Family History Society.

Woolwich and District Family History Society:
Metropolitan boroughs: Charlton; Plumstead; Woolwich.
Greater London boroughs: Greenwich.

Researchers should also consult appendix 2 for a breakdown of metropolitan boroughs, Greater London boroughs and family history societies arranged by parish. Each of these local family history societies has its own research and publication programmes, which the searcher interested in their area should be aware of. For example, London Westminster and North Middlesex Family History Society is producing a series of volumes on each area within its compass, generically entitled 'Researching in ...'.

Nor should researchers neglect local history societies, many of which have published source material and histories of their areas of interest. The local borough archives are the best place to enquire about such societies, the details of secretaries, etc. being subject to rapid change.

CHAPTER THREE
Registrar-General's records

T he Registrar-General's records of births, marriages and deaths are familiar, at least in concept, to every genealogist. Because of the expense of obtaining certificates and the even greater expense if they have to be obtained by post, much research has been baulked. However, often this is not necessary.

Firstly, access can now be gained to the indexes online, the references obtained, then the certificates can be ordered also online. The contemporary manuscript and typescript indexes are available without charge on the Ancestry website **http://www.ancestry.com/** . The certificate ordering service is at **http://www.gro.gov.uk/gro/content/certificates/** .

Furthermore, the indexes for the Victorian and Edwardian periods are being keyed in by volunteers and are freely searchable at the FreeBMD website **http://www.freebmd.org.uk/** . Coverage varies, but is growing rapidly and is virtually complete until the 1930s. The FreeBMD organisers are moving on to later periods. The availability of the indexes in electronic form enables some searches to be made that are not possible in the old manual ones and all are made physically easier than manhandling the huge volumes of the original indexes. Both Ancestry.com and FindMyPast are making available their own indexes from 1916-2005, but only of course to

subscribers – though an increasing number of libraries, such as the Society of Genealogists, subscribe to make them available to searchers.

In addition the records themselves are in the process of being digitised and reindexed. It has been agreed that the new indexes will include mother's maiden name for births (currently not given pre-Sep quarter 1911), spouse's surname for marriages (currently only given from Mar 1912) and the age at death (currently not given pre-1866). However the original contractor failed in the task. At the time of writing (July 2010), while the contract has been awarded to another agency, it is unclear when the work will be completed.

The indexes to these events which used to be available in their original paper and parchment format at the Family Records Centre are now available on microfiche at the British Library, Westminster Archives and London Metropolitan Archives (hereafter LMA).

An idea can be gained from the indexes of the geographical spread of a surname; the rarer overall, the more likely it is to be concentrated in a few areas, but many names quite common in one region are far rarer elsewhere. Though most names are represented by a London branch or branches, it is extremely useful to have a guide as to where the family was likely to originate from. For marriages, the Free BMD organisers have enabled a search to be made of all entries on a given page of the register. If you know the christian name of one party and the christian and surname of the other, you can often, therefore pick out the desired entry. This saves a lot of time and money buying wrong certificates, and chasing down descendants through the female line who you might not wish to go to the expense of getting certificates for at all.

It is also possible to use the indexes in a different way, especially for marriage entries. Marriage entries in Civil Registration records are duplicates of church records, except for the relatively few Register Office weddings of this time. If, therefore, the desired marriage can be found in the church records, then there is no need to obtain a certificate. It will usually be possible then to obtain a print-out either online or from a film.

The Registrar General's indexes will supply the registration district and quarter (e.g. Mar 1878) in which the event took place. Two booklets published by West Surrey FHS[4] (available for consultation at or purchase from the Society) will supply the names of all the Church of England churches within that registration district at various times and the location of their registers. Even after nonconformists were allowed to celebrate marriages in their chapels, the vast majority of weddings took place in the Established Church. Thus the genealogist who has access to the record office is enabled to trade off time against money. Sadly, often, either time or money are necessary, and the genealogist who can afford neither will have to rely on locating others more fortunately placed, who are researching the same ancestral lines. When an entry of interest is discovered, the researcher should look at a few entries either way. Joint marriage of siblings was quite common, and siblings often married in the same church even at an interval of months or years, and many marriage registers even in London have relatively few entries, making such speculative searches worthwhile. When a marriage certificate has to be obtained (or is found among family papers, etc.), the church register should wherever possible still be examined, first to make sure no copying errors have crept in, and also for the possibility of sibling marriages referred to above.

This technique does work best with marriages. Birth and baptism are two very different things, and while usually one followed the other within a year or so, a far smaller proportion of people were baptised in the established church than were married there. There is also the phenomenon of late baptism. Every register in which birth dates were recorded has people baptised years, and in some cases many years, after they were born. In essence the technique does not work at all for deaths/burials except in the period before 1853, in which year burials ceased in almost all the metropolitan churchyards and burial in cemeteries became compulsory; however, burial in churchyards had been in steep decline since about 1840. This subject is treated in more detail in the chapter on parish registers.

However, it should be mentioned here that it is very easy to ignore an entry of interest in the death indexes, because the person concerned has moved to an area remote from the place where they are last known to be. This may very well be simply because they have moved back to their place of origin after a period in London, or they may have gone into an institution, etc. This is especially likely to happen to the researcher in the period before 1866, when ages are not given in the indexes. Two actual examples may illustrate the point.

A Richard Garner was known to have been born and married in Westminster, to have been in St Olave Southwark in the 1860s, and was located in the 1871 census. A search was conducted for all Richard Garners in the indexes of death from 1871 onwards. Only one Richard of roughly the right age was found, but he had died in Godstone Registration District in rural Surrey. A certificate was obtained, although it was thought unlikely to be correct, but it proved indeed to be the right entry. Richard had, unfortunately, gone mad and been incarcerated in the Metropolitan Asylum at Caterham, which parish is in Godstone registration district.

An even more valuable result came from research into the family of Edward Baskett. The only information known about him was the birth and subsequent baptism of a daughter in 1853 in Southwark, and his marriage at Ipswich in 1851. Unfortunately all efforts to locate him in the 1861 census failed. A search of all possible entries from 1853 in the death indexes revealed a number of possible entries. They were whittled down, it being assumed that the ones in the London area would be the most likely. However, none of the post-1866 entries proved correct. Pre-1865 entries (where the age is not given in the indexes) were not that numerous but represented a fairly expensive proposition if certificates were to be obtained for them all. One possible entry, however, showed the death to be in Tendring Registration District, which was in Essex, not far from Ipswich. This proved to be the correct certificate. Furthermore, subsequent research showed that Edward's ancestry was in neither Southwark nor Ipswich, but in the Tendring area.

This is not the place for an extended discussion of how to use the Registrar General's records to the best advantage, this being treated fully in most guides to basic genealogy. However, there are some specific points with regard to London. Many of the registration districts are quite confusing, especially to beginners. The parishes covered by a registration district are described in the booklets already mentioned, but some should be especially mentioned. St Geo E. (St George in the East) should not be confused with St Geo S. (St George Southwark). East London and West London are quite small areas flanking the City of London, which is itself referred to as London C. in the Registrar General's indexes.

CHAPTER FOUR
Census Returns

The census returns are, of course, important to every British genealogist. To the researcher in London, however, they are however of quite exceptional value, as they provide by far the best opportunity to trace the ancestor out of London, which must be the aim. No effort should be spared to find the ancestor not just in one census, but in all the available ones.

Though no central records giving names were kept of pre-1841 census returns, a number of the schedules from which the statistics were compiled were kept. They vary in detail but generally list the householder by name, and the number of other people in the household arranged by age group, sex and general category of occupation, e.g. agricultural, trade, etc. For areas where they survive they can provide crucial evidence, and a list of known surviving returns for the London area is appended below; it is pleasing to see one or two more have been found since the last edition. Some of these early returns have been printed or are available on CD-ROM. Those items previously at the Guildhall Library have been transferred to LMA. There they are being assigned new references, but I have for the moment only been able to give the old reference.

Year	Parish	Reference	Repository
1801	Bridewell	33423/1	LMA
1801?	Enfield	DRO4/D8/3	LMA
1801	St Helen Bishopsgate	6852	LMA
1801	St Nicholas Acons	4306	LMA
1801	St Sepulchre	3260/1-5	LMA
1801	Hampstead	SCL A/G/1	Camden Library
1801	Hendon	5	Barnet Archives
1801	St Margaret Westminster	E2867	Westminster Archives
1801	St Mary le Strand	G1050	Westminster Archives
1801	Chelsea	SR61	Chelsea Library
1801	Chiswick	F101	LMA/SG
1810	New Brentford	6	
1811	All Hallows Lombard Street	Ms 10784	LMA
1811	St Ann Blackfriars	Ms 7753	LMA
1811	St Bartholomew the Less		St Bartholomew's Hospital
1811	St Benet Paul's Wharf	Ms 8933	LMA
1811	St Benet Sherehog	Ms 7626	LMA
1811	St Botolph Bishopsgate	Ms 4523	LMA
1811	St John the Baptist	Ms 7618	LMA
1811	St Mary Woolchurch Haw	Ms 8110	LMA
1811	St Mary Woolnoth	Ms 8109	LMA
1811	St Nicholas Acons	Ms 4306	LMA
1811	St Peter Cornhill	Ms 4190	LMA
1811	St Peter Paul's Wharf	Ms 8932	LMA
1811	St Sepulchre	Mss 3260/1-5	LMA
1811	St Swithin & St Mary Bothaw	Mss 566/1-2	LMA
1811	St Thomas Apostle	Ms 674	LMA
1811	Hackney	HAD7	Hackney Archives
1811	Hampstead	SCL A/G/2	Camden Library
1811	Hendon	5	Barnet Archives
1811	St Margaret Westminster	E2867	Westminster Archives
1811	St Mary le Strand	G1051	Westminster Archives
1821	All Hallows Lombard Street	Ms 10785	LMA
1821	Bridewell	Ms 33423/2	LMA
1821	St Benet Paul's Wharf	Ms 8934	LMA
1821	St Benet Sherehog	Ms 7627	LMA
1821	St Catherine Coleman	Ms 7723	LMA
1821	St Helen Bishopsgate	Ms 11419	LMA
1821	St Margaret Lothbury	Ms 4620	LMA
1821	St Mary Abchurch	Ms 3897	LMA

Year	Parish	Reference	Repository
1821	St Mary Woolchurch Haw	Ms 8110	LMA
1821	St Mary Woolnoth	Ms 8128	LMA
1821	St Nicholas Acons	Ms 4306	LMA
1821	St Peter Cornhill	Ms 4190	LMA
1821	St Sepulchre	Mss 3260/1-5	LMA
1821	St Swithin & St Mary Bothaw	Mss 3375/1-2	LMA
1821	St Thomas Apostle	Ms 674	LMA
1821	Hendon	5	Barnet Archives
1821	St Mary le Strand	G1052	Westminster Archives
1821	Hammersmith	PAH/1/214	Hammersmith Archives
1821	St Marylebone	8	Marylebone Library
1821	Poplar	POP/750-755[9]	Tower Hamlets Library
1821	Willesden	A50/1977	Grange Museum
1821	Hackney	P/J/CW/124[10]	Hackney Archives
1821	St Margaret Westminster	E2865	Westminster Archives
1831	St Benet Sherehog	Ms 8935	LMA
1831	St Catherine Cree	Ms 7697	LMA
1831	St Christopher le Stocks	Ms 6146	LMA
1831	St Clement Eastcheap	Ms 3681	LMA
1831	St Margaret Lothbury	Ms 4620	LMA
1831	St Mary Abchurch	Ms 3897	LMA
1831	St Mary Woolchurch Haw	Ms 8131	LMA
1831	St Mary Woolnoth	Ms 8128	LMA
1831	St Mathew Friday Street	Ms 7684	LMA
1831	St Nicholas Acons	Ms 4306	LMA
1831	St Peter Cornhill	Ms 4190	LMA
1831	St Peter Paul's Wharf	Ms 8932A	LMA
1831	St Peter Westcheap	Ms 7690	LMA
1831	St Thomas Apostle	Ms 674	LMA
1831	Friern Barnet		Barnet Archives
1831	Hammersmith	PAH/1/215	Hammersmith Archives
1831	St Marylebone	11	Marylebone Library
1831	Poplar	POP/756-67	Tower Hamlets Library
1831	Willesden	A57/1977	Grange Museum
1831	Harrow	DRO 3/F 13/1-5	LMA
1831	Hackney	P/J/Misc 1/1[12]	Hackney Archives
1831	Little Stanmore	E1 Extra Oversize	Harrow Library

Again, this is not the place to discuss the general techniques of using the census returns, but some special features apply in London. Firstly, the sheer difficulty of finding a person at all in the vast area of London has daunted many a researcher. This difficulty has been substantially reduced by the existence of online indexes.

The 1881 census was the first to be indexed. The index was the work of hundreds of volunteers using print-outs of the films supplied by the LDS Church who also co-ordinated the work with local family history societies and sorted the result. Research on people who were alive in that year was transformed by the availability of this index. It has also been used to show surname distribution over the whole country for that year. One may check the distribution for any given surname on the website: **http://www.spatial-literacy.org/UCLnames/**.

For all years 1841-1901 there are several online resources available; currently only FindMyPast has 1911 indexed. It is both an advantage and a disadvantage that, by and large, each pay-per-view provider has commissioned their own transcription. These vary widely in quality. I tested these, and, as at late 2006, Origins was quite clearly the most inclusive and accurate site. Unfortunately, they only have 1841, 1861 and 1871 available online. Most of the transcription was done abroad. The exception is The Genealogist, where much of the transcription and indexing was done by volunteers. A crosscheck showed, perhaps surprisingly, that there were more errors in this work than that done by paid assistance, however this is likely to be very variable.

Some census indexers have mistaken middle names for surnames, and misreading of Victorian handwriting is frequent and sometimes comical. One man with a very common name and therefore difficult to trace was however a photographer. However, the first website used had him listed as a 'philosopher' – an unlikely occupation in Mile End! It is not unknown for an indexer to miss a whole family or even frame of census. In an ideal world all indexes to the census should be checked, such as is possible at the Society of Genealogists' Library.

If you are researching an unusual surname, it is well worth looking at all the counties in the censuses, both to obtain a likely area of origin, and possibly to pick up some clues to actual ancestry. It must be remembered that migration was not necessarily a one-way street, always to London. Therefore, it may well be that a person in London in the nineteenth century may have returned to his or her home district (or the district to which his or her children had migrated) in old age, and by finding them in a census a birthplace may be identified.

Having found an entry of interest, the researcher, should always look at the original entry, as there is always the possibility of information coming not merely from other people of the same surname, but from people who have different surnames from the person being researched. One of the commonest cases is where a twice-widowed mother is living with a son by the first marriage, but there are many other possibilities, such as married daughters, sisters, nephews, nieces, cousins, etc.

It frequently happens that the researcher has an address as starting information for a census search. This will most normally come from a birth, marriage or death certificate, but may come from a variety of other sources. If it does come from a certificate, there will be the advantage of the registration district being given. In any case, the researcher will want to discover the civil parish and registration district in which the street, etc., was located.

There are several works which will help here. Streets in the City are keyed to their parishes in one West Surrey FHS booklet. Smaller places in the City are listed but not usually directly linked to their parish in H.A. Harben's Dictionary of London (1918) available online at: **www.british-history.ac.uk**. Another such West Surrey FHS booklet[13] provides a simple gazetteer to the Metropolis outside the City, keyed to parish references. In cases of difficulty, reference may need to be made to the Survey of Streets published by the London County Council. Editions appeared in 1901, 1912, 1929 and 1955. The 1912 edition is probably the most useful not just for streets, but also changes in their names; many names such as George Street, John Street and William Street occurred in many places, and often these places would be renamed to avoid confusion. If not understood such changes can cause confusion to contemporary researchers. The 1929 edition has been reproduced on CD-ROM[14].

The best CD source has recently been published by West Surrey FHS[15]. It contains the six Board School Maps of London, produced in 1906/7 by the London Schools Authorities. They were based on the 6" Ordnance Survey stock of the time and over printed with boundaries of the areas used in controlling the schools and also with the actual schools. To provide an index into the maps, a Street Index (published by West Surrey FHS as RA 44-46) designed for the 1:2500 Alan Godfrey Maps has been included and an index to all the schools in the overlay. You can go directly from the index to the locality on the appropriate map. The 'London County Council List of the Streets and Places' published in 1912 is also included on this CD. This includes all the streets as at that date, plus a list of abolished street names. There is no direct link from this to the maps, but a Reference Map is included to assist.

Do not be too concerned with the street number given in your reference. These could easily change. Indeed, if you do not find members of a family in the street where you expect to, then search at least the whole of the sub-district where you thought to find them. Movement among the urban population, especially the poor, was extremely rapid, often, indeed, 'one step ahead of the rentman'. You must be prepared for disappointment and will certainly need to persevere.

What do you do when you have found an ancestor in the census? The first thing in London, at least, should be to search at least the sub-district surrounding the entry for others of the same name if the ancestral birthplace revealed is not a rural one. The reason is that people did not come to London into a vacuum. They frequently moved at the suggestion or invitation of relatives and usually chose at least their first residence in the metropolis close to them. Equally, elderly people sometimes came to London at the end of their life to be near, but not necessarily in the same household as, their children. When indexing the 1851 census for Stepney, it was noticed that quite often unusual surnames which would appear only twice or three times in the whole index of nearly 100,000 people, appeared very close together in the films. Investigation of a few examples made it clear that in most cases this was no coincidence but that the people concerned were related. It is much easier to search using this technique now the censuses are name-indexed; indeed the whole registration district for the surname concerned should be searched, unless it is very common indeed.

It is often informative to search out witnesses on marriage certificates. They are often relatives even if of a different surname, and even non-relatives may be friends and come from the same rural area as the main person of interest. The same idea applies, of course, to any other persons found associated with the family of interest, who may be related or come from the same area, such as will beneficiaries, etc.

The facility is available on some of online sites to search by birthplace. Again, it can be extremely useful, once one has identified an ancestor as being born in a small place in the country, to search neighbouring areas for people born in the same place. Coincidences do happen, of course, but generally such people will be related, sometimes only by ties of friendship, but often by ties of kinship, too, and just occasionally truly unique information may result. For example, take the situation where the originally-found person is stated to have been born in a small Suffolk village. A few folios away is his sister, married and, therefore, with a different surname, but born in the same Suffolk village. However, living with her is the mother of both siblings, remarried, so again with a different surname, and born in a completely different place. It might otherwise be very difficult to establish her birthplace.

LMA does not hold films of the London returns; however it does provide free access to Ancestry.com so the years 1841-1901 are available.

It is often useful to consult maps of the area when using a census return. This can usually be best accomplished at the appropriate local borough archives centre which will normally have the census returns for its area (and any indexes compiled to them) and a good set of local Ordnance Survey and other maps. Many these days will have Internet access making wider searches possible. However, many late nineteenth century Ordnance Survey maps of local areas in London have been reprinted (and are available from the Society of Genealogists and other stockists) - searchers should certainly acquire copies of these for their areas of interest. Inexpensive indexes of places to these reproductions have been produced[16]. Also others have appeared on CD (see above).

CHAPTER FIVE

Parish and non-parochial registers and records

In some ways parish registers in London do not have the same supreme importance to genealogical research as they do in the rest of the country, as they will virtually never give the origins of the family. There is also a bewildering number of register series in London. However, they are, of course, still extremely important as sources.

There are two major repositories for parish registers in London, and a number of minor ones. Parish registers for the City of London which used to be at the Guildhall Library are now normally to be seen at LMA where the majority of London registers are held. Of the City parishes, only All Hallows Barking is still with the incumbent, but filmed by the LDS church with a copy of the film at LMA, while St Bartholomew the Less is at St Bartholomew's Hospital Archives (but the Guildhall Library and the Society of Genealogists both hold a complete transcript).

Most parish registers from the City of Westminster are to be found in the City of Westminster Archives Centre in St Ann's Street. Though St Margaret Westminster registers are at the Westminster Abbey Muniment Room, microfilm copies are available at the City of Westminster Archives Centre.

Deposited registers of parishes outside the City of Westminster are mainly to be found at LMA. Their collection of ancient registers is comprehensive; only a very few ancient parishes have not deposited their registers. Of these few, all except St Giles in the Fields (where the records are still at the church but with films at LMA) have had full transcripts made of at least their pre-1837 registers which may be consulted at either the Society of Genealogists, LMA or both, or are deposited at a borough record office. Hammersmith and Fulham Archives holds Hammersmith registers, and Greenwich and Lewisham hold some registers of a number of parishes in their area (of some of which there are films/transcripts at LMA). There are, however, a few parishes founded in Victorian times or later which have yet to deposit any registers, though new deposits are being made all the time. A telephone call should be made before a visit to ensure that any given register is both deposited and available for consultation, many registers having been deposited in a condition rendering them unfit to be produced, and there is a very long backlog of repair work. Parish maps of the area (and indeed of all England, Scotland and Wales) and simple lists of deposited pre-1837 registers are provided by the 'Phillimore Atlas'[17].

Non-register material is not necessarily as easy to locate as that, however. Even material that is at LMA may have come in from non-ecclesiastical parish sources and therefore not be listed with the registers. Much other material, being classified as civil parish records, has been deposited with the archive services of the various Boroughs. There is a brief listing to all this material available[18]

Most LMA catalogues have also been entered on a2a (**http://www.a2a.org.uk/**). However, it can still be difficult to find the records you want as the a2a search engine is so large. To give an example if you enter St Olave Southwark in a2a it produces (as at July 2010) 893 references, of which no less than 231 are at LMA. There has, however, an immense improvement in the a2a site organisation which groups entries and fairly easily enables the researcher to find the parish registers, if that is what they want, even though they are listed as St Olave, Bermondsey!

If you do find the parish of interest on a2a, it is worth clicking on 'Catalogue Table of Contents', which will provide a detailed list of the archives. The button 'Catalogue in Full' provides just that and is far too voluminous for 99% of searchers. If you do press the 'in Full' button, don't press print unless you really need it all, as there may be dozens of pages to a file, and not a few have over a hundred. LMA themselves have a database of their major genealogical material called 'London Generations' (**http://www.cityoflondon.gov.uk/corporation/family-research/ registerSearchForm.asp**). To use this properly you really need to know the Borough your parish of interest was in (and remember to extend 'St' to 'Saint'!). It does give some useful detail (like microfilm numbers) not always available on a2a, but is far from being either comprehensive or consistent in its choice of records to include. Similarly, LMA have put their catalogue online. Again, one tends to be overwhelmed by the number of possibilities for a search, but patience can be rewarded by some unexpected gems.

In the medieval period, almost all the inhabitants of the area now known as London lived in either the City of London or the City of Westminster. Gradually, however, the population overspilled, to Southwark on the south bank (which is in the ancient county of Surrey), filling in the area between the two cities, and outwards. The outward movement continued beyond the old Surrey boundary into Deptford and Greenwich in Kent, and beyond the Middlesex one into Essex. For this reason, searchers may have to consider not only London and Middlesex sources, but also Surrey and even Kent and Essex ones.

Beginning in the early eighteenth century, the cities themselves started to have more and more non-residential buildings such as shops, offices and warehouses. Parishes could be wholly or virtually wholly swallowed up as was St Christopher le Stocks by the Bank of England in 1780, and St Katharine by the Tower by St Katharine's Dock in 1825. Gradually, therefore, the population of these central areas fell. The population of London, however, continued grow rapidly, the growth coming in the suburbs. There was a repeated demographic pattern in ever-widening (and more or less concentric) rings as London developed: swift population expansion was followed by stagnation, in turn followed by fall or even collapse.

By the nineteenth century, therefore, the population of the City of London was small, and falling, while such areas as St Marylebone in the west, Shoreditch in the north, Stepney in the east and Bermondsey in the south were growing rapidly. The central areas were being depopulated because more and more houses were either being demolished for, or converted to, commercial or industrial purposes.

At first the pattern of church provision changed only very little due to vested interests. Parish churches in the City generally had small and declining congregations, only partially offset by the demolition of churches themselves for commercial development. The suburban ancient parish churches could not hope to cater adequately for the vast numbers of inhabitants. A few new parishes were created in the seventeenth and eighteenth centuries such as Christ Church Southwark (1670) and St Luke Old Street (1733), but there were far too few of them. In the nineteenth century new churches started to be built from the 1820s in increasing numbers, due as much as anything else to a revival in the Church of England's desire to evangelise the population, encouraged by the growing success of nonconformists in winning converts.

Researchers need to be aware of these developments as, particularly in Victorian times, vital events may have taken place in a number of daughter parish churches.

The Church of Jesus Christ of Latter-Day Saints filmed virtually all the registers which used to be at the Guildhall Library. It has also filmed a large number of registers at LMA, but its coverage there is far less comprehensive, and it has filmed very little at Westminster at all. This patchiness is reflected in the coverage of the International Genealogical Index (IGI) for London and Middlesex, a well-known source compiled by the LDS church and which contains mainly baptisms, though there are some marriages. The City of London has very good coverage, but the suburbs and Westminster are quite weak. Indications of coverage with LDS batch numbers can be found online at **http://freepages.genealogy.rootsweb.com/ ~hughwallis/IGIBatchNumbers/CountyLondon_including_Middlesex_(A-M).htm** .

In partial compensation for this, LMA assembled a team of volunteers to index its registers. The team concentrated on, roughly, 1770-1837, though there are indexes to other periods. Indexes to burials are rare, but most of the larger parishes have indexes to baptisms and marriages for much or all of this period. The indexes were almost all compiled one to each volume of the register, so there are a large number of indexes to each parish and no overall indexes to long sequences of years. These indexes have now been fiched or filmed, and some of the originals donated to the Society of Genealogists. LMA is open Monday to Friday during office hours, on most Tuesdays and Thursdays to 7.45 p.m. (though a prior appointment is necessary for some material). It also opens on some Saturdays. Intending Saturday searchers should check specifically for any given day.

The comprehensiveness of the IGI for the City of London, together with the availability of LDS films at their Family History Centres, makes research in the City of London far easier. The IGI is available in the Guildhall Library and at LMA both on microfiche, on CD-ROM and on-line.

For marriages there are several indexes, of which the two most important are Boyd's Marriage Index and the Pallot Index. Boyd's Index is a vast series of typescript indexes (to all England) containing several million marriages compiled by the late Percival Boyd and various helpers. The index is organised in county divisions and in periods (mainly twenty-five year sections). The originals are at the Society of Genealogists, and there are full microfilm copies of them at Salt Lake City and thus available through Family History Centres. A copy of the London and Middlesex section is also available at the Guildhall Library. Boyd took the bulk of his index entries from printed registers, and is therefore strongest for the pre-1754 period, though many large parishes are covered right up to 1837. The index has been rekeyed and the results are available on the Origins website[19]. Members of the Society of Genealogists have special terms of access. Work is underway to produce supplements to Boyd's Index filling some of the remaining gaps in online availability. The Society has produced a list of the parishes covered by Boyd's Index and this is available online at Origins.

For the period 1780-1837, the Pallot Index is extremely useful. This vast index is held by the Institute of Heraldic and Genealogical Studies, Northgate, Canterbury, Kent. It contains a huge proportion of London marriages between 1780 and 1837, the period 1800-1837 being especially comprehensive. It contains some entries from parish registers that have since been destroyed and for which, therefore, it is a unique source. There is also a much less comprehensive Baptisms index for the same period. These indexes have been keyed onto two CD-ROMs and issued by Ancestry.Com. Ancestry has also made them available on their website. Using the CD-ROMs, one can key from an entry onto the Net and view the original slip. While there are many omissions and inaccuracies (some, frankly, quite grotesque) in the work as it appears on the CD-ROM, it is a source which finds many otherwise 'impossible' marriages. Due to the extremely poor rekeying, a search in Pallot online must never, however, be regarded as remotely covering the parishes indexed into the original slip index.

At the Institute above there is also Father Anstruther's index to Catholic Marriages 1700-1870, which covers some sixty London Roman Catholic parishes; this index has been reproduced on CD-ROM by the Parish Register Transcription Society (**www.prtsoc.org.uk/**) from whom it is available.

Despite the 1754 act, people continued to marry more or less where they pleased, often obtaining no more than the minimum residence requirement. Even after 1754, some places were very popular for weddings, and contain more marriage entries than their population would warrant. Examples include St Leonard Shoreditch, St John at Hackney, St James Piccadilly, St George Hanover Square and St Mary Magdalen Fish Street.

Many though by no means all, City of London registers have been published (chiefly by the Harleian Society) or have typescript transcripts at the Society of Genealogists and/or the Guildhall Library. The printed and transcribed ones tend to be the smaller inner parishes, not the larger outer ones such as St Giles Cripplegate, St Botolph Aldgate and St Andrew Holborn, though their baptisms are almost all included in the IGI. The Society of Genealogists' website has a regularly updated list of register copies which it holds which should always be consulted, as it is a lot easier to consult an indexed copy than an original. However, the Society has relatively poor holdings of the big urban parishes, since the transcription and indexing of these is such a monumental task.

One of the most besetting faults of genealogists is a failure to search for the burial of ancestors. This fault has been exacerbated by over-reliance on the IGI which, of course, contains no burials. Especially after 1813 when ages are uniformly given in the registers, it is quite essential to do so, and indeed to trace all the brothers and sisters, too, wherever possible, as clues as to origins can arise and a reasonably accurate year of birth is often a prerequisite for going further back. A burial index (compiled by the author) for the central parishes in the City area for the period 1813-1853 is available on microfiche[20] and is available on the Origins and FindMyPast websites. Monnica Stevens has extended the work to some of the cemeteries in the London area, and indexes are available to Tower Hamlets, Bunhill Fields and Spa Fields Cemeteries, all very well-frequented places of burial. These are also available on the FindMyPast website. These pieces of work are on the latest edition of the National Burial Index which is rather more useful for London than it used to be but still very weak. Miss Stevens is extending her work to the 1754-1812 period, and pre-1754 is being rekeyed in a project organised by the writer.

For the period before 1813, Boyd's London burials should be consulted. As with Mr Boyd's work on marriages, this index relied heavily on printed registers, and only lists adult males, but it is a useful finding aid even as a bit of a 'lucky dip' and is now available online on the Origins website, together with Boyd's London Citizens, another compilation of the indefatigable Percival Boyd, which puts together various references to London freemen.

Nonconformists had always had their burial grounds, but beginning in the 1830s a greater and greater proportion of Anglican burials was in cemeteries. After 1853, when most London churchyards were closed to further burials for health reasons, almost all Londoners were buried in cemeteries. Huge areas were set aside for cemeteries; in particular, the Brookwood Cemetery at Woking in Surrey had a special railway service carrying corpses from London in vast numbers. There seems little rhyme or reason in the choosing of a place of burial and this can be extremely difficult to find. London cemeteries and their records are listed in a guide[21].

A relatively new online pay per view resource is putting digitised cemetery records online. To be found at **https://www.deceasedonline.com/** it currently (July 2010) has material from Alperton, Hampstead, Hornchurch, Rainham, Trent Park, Upminster, Wembley and Willesden cemeteries, but may be expected to grow rapidly.

The area outside the City of London has very few printed or typescript transcripts, though some have appeared from time to time. Even these tend, naturally enough, to be of the earliest registers, which are the least used by the average genealogist. Published editions have appeared of some Westminster registers and of early St James Clerkenwell, for example. Some marriage registers such as St Marylebone (to 1812) and St George Hanover Square (to 1837) have been printed to quite late dates. However, many of the parishes have either no transcript at all, or only of the very earliest periods.

The daunting size of the average London register precludes any realistic hope of printing them in full. It has been the hope for some while that digitisation will be the key to making these records available. The experience of census returns shows that indexing can be done at least as accurately overseas as by volunteers in this country. Some will regret that indexes so produced will be done so commercially and thus will require some subscription or fee for access, and that they will only be available on the Internet. Unfortunately, the alternative is no access at all for people who cannot get to London, and long and often fruitless searches for those who can.

The biggest online addition has been that recently Ancestry.com has added digitised images of the vast majority of the Anglican and nonconformist register holdings of the LMA (including those previously at the Guildhall Library). The material from 1813 onwards is indexed; that before not. Unfortunately, one has to say that the work has been done very poorly. While it is wonderful for researchers all round the world to be able to access images, Ancestry have confused the source of the information in many cases, with some extraordinary howlers. Thus parishes are completely wrongly named, allocated to the wrong borough, parishes south of the Thames are placed north of it, and vice versa. Half a register may be digitised and not the end of the book. Some registers have a few, seemingly random pages done only (e.g. Hayes 1557-1638 has just 18 frames available from a 200 folio register). Banns and marriages are confused and indeed conflated, as are Bishops' Transcripts. In addition, the quality of such indexing as has been done is lamentable. Altogether this is an opportunity lost. It has been necessary to do a lot of work merely to try to identify what has been done. The results are being posted on the West Surrey FHS as free downloads.

For Westminster, the City of Westminster Archives Centre is planning to digitise much of its collections, including the registers. This is likely to occur during the currency of this book.

Bishops' Transcripts are not a major source for London genealogy. A connected series only begins for most parishes in 1800, ending in the mid-nineteenth century.

27

Before 1800, most parishes have at most two or three years (for some reason 1629-30 and 1639-40 being by far the most common survivals) for which returns are extant. Most of what returns survive is in the same repository as the registers, though there are some small differences, and a few for areas in which the archbishop of Canterbury or his officials exercised so-called 'peculiar' jurisdiction are at Lambeth Palace Library. They do provide copies of much of the early nineteenth century registers of the Westminster area at LMA, and have been digitised by Ancestry. Some further details are given in the one of Jeremy Gibson's guides[22]. Comprehensive lists of Bishops' Transcripts year by year have appeared in the appropriate volumes of the National Index of Parish Registers[23].

Allegations and bonds for Marriage Licences survive in very large quantities for the Metropolitan area, and from several courts. LMA has produced an index on CD-ROM for the period 1771-1837 for those allegations for licences made to the bishop of Winchester whose diocese, until the mid-nineteenth century, included most of what is now south London. The period before 1771 for this court has a printed index[24]. Searchers should note that only one allegation survives between 1692 and 1724. This work is available reproduced on microfiche from West Surrey FHS[25]. LMA has now made an index available online for the whole period 1673-1850 in its London Signatures feature **http://www.cityoflondon.gov.uk/corporation/wills/engine/wills_search.asp** which allows the searcher to order a scan of the original which will usually have at least some extra information. The Society of Genealogists has produced on fiche basic surname to surname indexes for the periods unprinted to the two great national series of marriage licence allegations, the Faculty Office and the Vicar-General's series, both preserved at Lambeth Palace Library. These latter indexes are available on the Origins website.

Most London nonconformist registers, as those for other places, were deposited with the Registrar-General in 1837 (National Archives class RG 4), and a few some twenty years later and subsequently (National Archives class RG 8). They have been filmed by the LDS church and baptisms from the films have been abstracted and indexed into the IGI. Apart from Quaker registers, there are virtually no marriages in the series, since, apart from the Quakers (and the Jews who refused to surrender their registers), all marriages were supposed to be in the Anglican church after 1754, and in practice most were so solemnised before that date. Even after 1837, most nonconformists married in either the local Anglican church or the local Register Office. LMA has a large collection of deposited nonconformist registers, mostly baptisms, though there are large numbers of twentieth century Methodist marriage registers. A few of these registers predate 1837, but most begin in the mid-nineteenth century or later.

For each major denomination, the Society of Genealogists has produced a volume in its 'My Ancestor was ...' series. These are essential reading for anyone researching nonconformist ancestry, as is Michael Gandy's list of Catholic registers for people with Catholic ancestry[26]. Many Catholic registers have been printed by the Catholic Record Society, which is fortunate, because there was no parochial system for Catholics until recently, and registers were kept covering very large areas by itinerant priests. Some areas of London had few Protestant nonconformists, e.g. Rotherhithe; other areas such as Hackney had large concentrations of dissenters. Similarly, Catholics (and even more Jews) tended to congregate in a few areas, such as the Catholic centres in Southwark and St Marylebone, and the Jewish settlements in Whitechapel, and later Finchley and Stoke Newington.

Falling in a slightly separate category are the records of the 'Foreign Churches'. The large majority of these were Huguenot churches, established as places of worship for Protestant refugees from Europe, principally France and the Low Countries. The number of these churches grew rapidly after 1685, with the Revocation of the Edict of Nantes, and the end of religious toleration in France for over a century. Originally, their records were all in the language of the refugees, principally French, though there were churches using Dutch and German too. Fortunately for the searcher, these registers have virtually all been printed by the Huguenot Society of London and others. The marriages from these are all available on the Origins website. The Huguenot Society of London has published a large amount of other source material, and maintains a library with many manuscript collections at University College, London. This is open to non-members on payment of a fee, currently £10 per day.

Among the holdings of the National Archives are several large series of registers. The most likely place for the burial of more prosperous London nonconformists was Bunhill Fields burial ground, and for poorer ones, Gibraltar Row burial ground. A list is provided in Tracing Your Ancestors in the National Archives. An excellent index is available to Gibraltar Row, and to Bunhill, as mentioned above, there is an index at the Society of Genealogists and on fiche. The National Archives also holds two series of general birth registers for nonconformists. Nonconformists often found great difficulty if the need arose to find evidence of birth date or parentage, either because parents did not baptise their children at all, or because nonconformist register-keeping (which was non-statutory) was always considerably scrappier and more liable to loss than that of the Anglican church which was regulated by law. In 1742, therefore, a registry was established called Dr Williams' Registry which, while not limited to nonconformists, was largely used by them, to register the births of children. Its records have been deposited, as have the smaller records of a similar registry established by the Methodist church in 1829. Both organisations ceased to register after the advent of Civil Registration in 1837. Both registries have been filmed by the Latter-Day Saints and indexed entries are included amongst much other material on a LDS CD-ROM entitled Vital Records Index - British Isles.

Also deposited at the National Archives (where they constitute class RG 7) are the Fleet Registers. These are registers and notebooks kept by people conducting clandestine marriages within the Fleet prison and in buildings in the vicinity. There are several hundred of them bearing dates from the third quarter of the seventeenth century to 1754, when such marriages were stamped out by the application of Hardwicke's Marriage Act. In the generation before 1754, the Fleet registers are not merely a source to be looked at for marriages; they are the most likely place to find a marriage not found in the normal parishes of the parties. This is not limited to London people. Men and women came from all over England, but especially the south-east, to the Fleet for marriage without formality. Some selected indexes do exist at the National Archives and elsewhere, but an overall index to the Fleet Marriages is extremely desirable. A number of other places were centres for irregular marriages before 1754 such as St James Duke's Place and Holy Trinity in the Minories. This difficult area for research is the subject of a book[27].

However, once again, the situation has been transformed by digitisation. The Genealogist (**http://www.thegenealogist.co.uk/**) has digitised all the non-conformist material at the National Archives (including the Fleet marriages) and it is available at their pay per view site. Ancestry has recently completed the digitisation of the nonconformist material at LMA. A guide to the London and Middlesex nonconformist material and digitised by Ancestry.com has been published by the author and can be found online as Research Aid 53 on the West Surrey FHS website. Bunhill Fields and one or two other cemeteries are available on FindMyPast.

The National Index of Parish Registers volume for London and Middlesex provides a full list of all known registers, non-parochial registers, Bishops' Transcripts and modern copies where the church or chapel was founded in 1837 or before. The LMA and Guildhall Library have both produced printed lists of registers they hold (the Guildhall ones now of course being at LMA), and City of Westminster Archives Centre has a list available; all these lists are available online.

Monumental inscriptions exist in very large numbers in the London area; however, the percentage of people with surviving inscriptions is very low, and the proportion of these which have been copied is also low. However, several local Family History

Societies have published lists of burials or monumental inscriptions. London Westminster and North Middlesex Family History Society having been particularly active in the field of copying church and churchyard inscriptions. There is a published list of monumental inscription copies for Middlesex[28], and another for the Surrey parishes[29].

With an uncommon name, the London researcher should consult the IGI for the whole country. He can thereby gauge the frequency with which the name is to be found in any area. In the case of very uncommon names, he may discover that virtually all holders of the name come from one or two areas of the country, sometimes quite small areas. Even christian names can give a clue; Marmaduke and (to a lesser extent) Solomon are far more frequently met with in Yorkshire than anywhere else. An extreme example might be provided by an ancestor of unknown origin called Marmaduke Micklethwaite, a case I have come across! All such clues need to be followed up methodically and ruthlessly.

City of London parishes seem to have hoarded their material considerably more than the average rural parish. This means that such records as churchwardens' accounts, vestry minutes and various inhabitants' lists survive in great profusion and from very early dates. For the period when the City is most likely to be the area being researched (i.e. before 1800) they can be accessed by several Guildhall Library guides[30]. These sorts of records outside the City area are listed in one of the West Surrey FHS guides[31] and in the relevant leaflets published by London and North Middlesex FHS.

CHAPTER SIX
Directories, lists of taxpayers, voters & other name-lists

From the late eighteenth century on increasingly comprehensive directories were produced by such firms as Kelly's Directories, Ltd.

It must be stated immediately however, that the poorer districts of London never had directories compiled for them, or such as were only included a tiny proportion of the inhabitants. The principal purposes of directories were to list tradesmen for their customers and vice-versa. Thus most directories have a section called the 'Court Directory' listing the better-off inhabitants. Another section lists the tradesmen under the various trades and another lists householders street by street. Directories vary in this, a few having no alphabetical list at all.

Some directories, such as Boyle's Court Guides, Royal Red Books and Royal Blue Books concentrated on the top echelon of society, to the exclusion of tradespeople. Other directories concentrated exclusively on a profession, or later a trade. Lists of clergymen and medical directories were the first, but by the end of the nineteenth century many other occupations had their own directories too. A useful book provides a listing of these[32].

The Guildhall Library has an unrivalled collection of directories covering the whole country, but, as might be expected from its location, with particular strength in the London area. It has also greatly benefited from the deposit of Kelly's own reference archive of directories. Other large collections are held at LMA, City of Westminster Archives Centre and at the Bishopsgate Institute. Most local libraries and archive centres have collections, some very substantial, of directories of their area. Indeed a bibliography which listed all known London directories[33] shows that a very large number of directories are known from a single copy. Simplified and inexpensive listings of directories of places in the ancient counties of Middlesex and Surrey are available[34].

A number of directories have appeared online on a most useful site **http://www.historicaldirectories.org/hd/index.asp**. They can be browsed or searched. Unfortunately this initiative is not continuing its work. The following are the London and Middlesex ones available:

Kelly's (or Post Office) London 1808, 1841, 1852, 1882, 1884, 1891, 1895, 1896, 1899, 1901, 1904, 1905, 1906, 1907, 1908, 1910, 1911, 1914, 1915, 1916, 1917, 1918
Kelly's Ealing, Acton etc. 1889/90, 1893/4, 1907, 1911, 1914
Mason's Brentford, Kew 1853
Webster's Red Book 1897

Many directories are being reproduced by such firms as Archive CD Books (now continuing as Archive CD Books Ireland) for sale on CD-ROM.

Directories may be used for a number of purposes. They are good indicators of movement, though they tended to lag, sometimes substantially, behind actual movements. Researchers will sometimes find ancestors, known to be deceased, plying their trades posthumously in Kelly's for some years, but in general it is surprising how good directory information is.

Directories can supply addresses from which census records, parish registers, etc. may be researched. If a tradesman is shown with both a private and a business address, naturally both must be searched. It is easy to miss this, however, if the private and business addresses are in separate directories, as may often happen.

Records of voters are a similar source. Poll books are printed lists of the votes actually cast at elections. In general only a very small proportion of the population enjoyed the vote before 1832, and for nearly fifty years after male suffrage was far from universal. Poll books appear to survive for the County of Middlesex for 1705, 1713, 1715, 1750, 1768, 1769, 1772, 1802 and for parts of the county for 1806 and

1820. For the City of London there are poll books for 1682, 1710, 1713, 1717, 1722, 1724, 1727, 1734, 1768, 1771, 1772, 1773, 1781, 1784, 1792, 1796, 1831 and 1837, with numerous poll books relating to only one ward or parish. Westminster (which had a wider early suffrage than most constituencies) has poll books for 1749, 1774, 1780, 1784, 1788, 1790, 1796, 1802, 1806, 1818, 1819, 1820, 1837 and 1841. Poll books are listed in greater detail in one of Jeremy Gibson's guides[35]. Some of these poll books have been reprinted and a few are starting to appear online.

In the nineteenth century, electoral registers start to survive. For London they tend to be less useful than in rural areas, as they are almost universally organised by street, not alphabetically. An exception is the Voters List of 1871 which are in alphabetical order by ward for most places. They are, however, useful for determining more exactly than a directory when a move took place, and for gauging the likely age of a person by the first appearance. Without a massive indexing programme, however, they will remain mainly a very difficult primary source for addresses not known from other sources. There are excellent collections of Electoral Registers in the British Library, LMA, the Guildhall Library and in local record offices and reference libraries. As ever there is a published list of them by Jeremy Gibson[36].

For the period before the census returns, there are a huge number of listings of inhabitants compiled for various different reasons, though most frequently for some sort of revenue-raising. Rates were raised for the relief of the poor and the maintenance of the church, the highways and later for providing lighting and other municipal purposes. Central taxes were imposed on various things, including land and windows, and earlier lay subsidies were exacted to give revenue to the king. Records of all these sources survive in almost overwhelming profusion, especially for the City area.

A few of these miscellaneous lists are starting to appear online; for example a Tithe list of 1638 and the rate for 1693/4 are freely available on the British History site. The Association Oath Roll 1696 for the City of London has been printed by West Surrey FHS[37] and is available on the Origins website. However, the information given by any individual list is usually fairly limited though if a sequence of such lists can be compared they can hold much greater evidential value, especially as to movement. Unfortunately, in the absence of much more indexing of such material such a research method is usually not practicable and, in practice, the genealogist will probably be confined to using those sources made readily available by being printed or at least indexed. Four recent bibliographies provide guides to these[38].

CHAPTER SEVEN
Poor law records

The operation of the poor law must be divided into two periods, pre-
and post-1834. Prior to 1834, the 1601 poor law, though amended,
was still substantially in force. The 1601 Act had laid down the
principle of settlement. This notion (elements of which survived well into
this century) revolved round the idea that each parish should be responsible
for its own poor, and not for those of its neighbours. The theory was that
each person was 'settled in' a given parish (and therefore its
responsibility); all that had to be done was to discover which parish it was.
Strangely (and rather unfortunately from our point of view), birth in a
parish did not give a person a settlement unless they were born there
illegitimately or the father was deemed to be settled there and the child had
no subsequent settlement of its own.

Settlement could be gained in a number of ways. In practice, most
settlements were gained either by a person serving as a servant on a yearly
hiring, serving an apprenticeship, renting a tenement worth £10 per annum,
or else it was established by virtue of the person's father's settlement.
Children took their father's settlement until they obtained one of their own,
or, if their father's settlement was unknown, their mother's.

There were umpteen complications: people born in Ireland, Scotland or 'in
foreign parts' had no settlement in England. Because quite large sums of

money were involved, parish officials tried everything they knew to deny settlement in their parish. At first, parish officials had virtually blanket power to prevent a person remaining in their parish. This hindered movement to such an extent that in 1696 the law was changed to permit parishes to issue settlement certificates; these were legally enforceable and acknowledged that a given person or family were settled in the issuing parish. The parish to which the person went would keep the certificate in the parish chest as security and, if the person became 'chargeable' (i.e. needed to be relieved by the parish), they would be promptly returned to the parish of origin with a bill for the costs of their maintenance and removal. People moving around without such certificates were liable to immediate removal. Furthermore, if they were considered to be vagrants, a whipping followed. As an alternative to the settlement certificate, the parish might accept a bond of indemnity (indeed these can very occasionally predate the 1601 Act). These bonds were entered into by people the parish officials considered sufficiently well-off to meet the costs of relieving and removing the subject of the bond. Most of the people indemnifying under bonds were either related to the subject or his employer.

Not until 1795 was a law passed which allowed people freedom of movement provided they did not become chargeable. The onus thus fell even more on the parish officials to discover the settlement of their poor. They did this by means of the 'settlement examination'. The pauper was asked what his settlement was, and how it had been achieved. Settlement examinations did not begin in 1795; they had been used for many years, but they become much commoner at this time. Gradually, also, they tend to give more and more information. At their best, settlement examinations can give substantial biographical details about people who otherwise have left little personal information. However, analysis of a large number of London settlement examinations by the writer while abstracting them, shows that only a small proportion achieve what is most desired by the searcher, evidence of a move from a rural area.

When a pauper was to be removed, an order was obtained from Justices of the Peace by the parish officials. This order was known as the 'removal order' and gives the parish of origin and the parish to which the pauper is being sent, listing his family.

The ages of children are almost always given and the ages of the adults occasionally. In early ones, it is not uncommon for a small settlement examination to be included, and this was universally done if the pauper was accused of vagrancy. Justices of the Peace also approved apprenticeship indentures where the parish officials arranged for the apprenticing of pauper children. The idea was to ensure that the home was suitable; for example, Justices were known to refuse to allow the apprenticing of girls to alehouses. However, nothing prevented the fact that paupers were virtually always apprenticed to the most low paid trades, and were little more than serfs.

During the Napoleonic wars, records known as Militia Substitution Papers can be found. Selection for the Militia was by lot; however, someone so chosen could pay someone else to substitute for him. If the substitute was actually called up to service, however, his wife and children if he had any were entitled to parochial relief. The papers are useful for places of residence, and ages (and sometimes exact dates of birth) are given for the children.

Poor law records survive in profusion in some parish chests, while in others there are none whatever due to parochial clear-outs at some time or another. Many poor law records were classified as civil parish records and are to be found in borough archives rather than in LMA. Hand lists have been prepared and published by West Surrey FHS[39], indicating which parishes have what material. For the City of London there are several volumes of abstracts compiled by the author available at the Guildhall Library and at the Society of Genealogists. West Surrey FHS has published a complete calendar to the huge archive of St Botolph Aldgate settlement examinations[40]. Both this calendar, the author's earlier work and a new series of the vast St Sepulchre archive is also available online at Origins. More of this material will be added shortly. For the suburban area, the London and North Middlesex Family History Society has been particularly active in indexing these records.

Many accumulations remain uncalendared, however, though it may be expected that much more material will appear online in the next few years as LMA's contract with Ancestry.com includes this material, of which they have so far only produced a limited amount.

It must however be repeated that, valuable as these documents are, the movement recorded by them, prior to 1834 is usually short-scale and within the London area. It should also be noted that many poor law records are not deposited in the record offices where the registers of the parish are to be found. Since they were considered records of the civil (as opposed to the ecclesiastical) parish, they frequently ended up with the municipal, instead of the ecclesiastical, authorities, and these authorities deposited them in libraries, generally before the establishment of LMA's predecessor.

In 1834, however, there was a radical rethink. While the principle of settlement was retained, parishes were grouped into unions (though some London parishes were big enough to become single parish unions). These poor law unions developed separate records from parishes. They are listed for the whole country in four titles in Jeremy Gibson's series[3]. Furthermore, removal became much more restricted (a five year period of residence ensured irremovability), and, in 1876, removal as a physical fact was abolished, though parishes continued to have to pay for people who had been notionally 'removed' to them, well into the 20th century.

Some poor law union material seems to have strayed into the parish, some from the parish into the poor law union archive, and this has unfortunately resulted in some chaotic splits in archive groups, so, as with earlier material, some records of the nineteenth century may be found in libraries rather than LMA.

Settlement examinations after 1834, where they survive in either parochial or poor law union records, tend to be very full. This whole question is discussed and several examples given in an article in the *Genealogists' Magazine*[41]. They give information which may be unobtainable elsewhere. Frequently there are at least rough indexes to them, but they tend to be very under-utilised as a source for the nineteenth century.

An example given in the *Genealogists' Magazine* article based on a City of London parish's register of settlement examinations will perhaps illustrate the wealth of details which may be found. A man called Robert Clery is the examinee. He gives his age, wife's name and birthplace, which happened to be New York, where he says his father, a labourer, died. His mother Mary returned to County Cork when Robert was three years old. Many subsequent movements are given, together with details of both Robert's marriages, one of which was in a Catholic chapel, and of his children.

Considerable work is needed (and indeed planned) on London's post-1834 settlement material.

CHAPTER EIGHT
Wills and administrations

Wills are a major source for the London researcher as elsewhere. While, in general, wills assist a researcher in the wrong way, by going forward in time rather than back, they can provide a wealth of information about an individual and his family, which can tie them together firmly, which is often very difficult to do with the teeming populace of London.

After 1858, it is at least relatively easy to find if a will of interest exists. Yearly indexes to all wills proved in England and Wales exist at 1st Avenue House, High Holborn, and the indexes give enough information for one almost always to know whether a will is likely to be of interest. For uncommon surnames, a blanket examination of all wills of that surname can be a profitable exercise, not least in suggesting areas of origin for Londoners.

Unfortunately, there was a profusion of courts which could prove wills in the London area prior to 1858. After about 1750, however, most of these courts had a declining business. This was because more and more people were proving their wills in either the Prerogative Court of Canterbury (hereafter PCC) or the Consistory Court of London. It is easy to understand why there should be this growth in the PCC's business. It was the premier and most

prestigious court in the country and might be expected to keep its records best. In addition to this, for larger estates a PCC probate was essential; the Bank of England, for example, would accept no other. It is much more difficult to explain the very large growth in business at the Consistory Court, which by the early eighteenth century was only proving a very small number of wills, mostly those of clergymen. Suddenly, in the 1780s, it started proving a very large amount of business, and this high level continued until the abolition of ecclesiastical jurisdiction in early 1858.

The British Record Society, British Origins and the LDS Church have combined resources to begin a National Wills Index (which will also include administrations). It is planned that the index will be free, and then linked to the appropriate record office from which a scan of the original may be offered.

The records of the PCC are at the National Archives. There are full indexes to testators in them for the 1853-58 period, and then yearly calendars back to 1801. From 1750-1800, they are indexed in six volumes by Anthony Camp[42]. For the period 1701-1749, the Friends of the National Archives have compiled an index, available on fiche. Prior to 1700, there is a large series of printed indexes (mostly published by the British Record Society). However, work on the wills of this court has been transformed by their digitisation. The indexes are freely available online on the National Archives website and digitised images may be downloaded for a modest fee (indeed freely within the National Archives itself). At the National Archives itself images are available without charge. Currently this availability only extends to wills, not to administrations. The Genealogist pay per view site provides digitised images of the wills in well over 100 years of the PCC's life which may be freely downloaded by subscribers.

From 1796 duty was payable on many estates over a certain value. The scope of the duty was gradually increased and relatively few estates after 1812 escaped duty. Records of the Estate Duty Office are held at the National Archives. They include indexes (NA reference IR 27) and registers (NA references IR 26). The former indicate in which court a will was proved, the latter usually indicates a date of death. The records were often annotated for many years after the original entry was made, which may provide useful information, such as the later whereabouts of legatees. Therefore, for deaths after 1796, these records may be used to determine the court in which probate was granted.

For further guidance, the researcher should use Jeremy Gibson's invaluable guide on probate jurisdiction[43], not forgetting that the metropolitan area covered all of Middlesex, and parts of Essex, Surrey and Kent. A brief list of jurisdictions keyed to parishes is given in appendix 2. There is also an excellent leaflet produced by

LMA on this subject, and London and North Middlesex Family History Society has produced a guide to London wills.

Of the other major courts, the Consistory Court of London, Archdeaconry Court of Middlesex (Middlesex division), Archdeaconry Court of London and the Commissary Court of London records are at LMA. The British Record Society has indexes in print or in progress for the period up to 1700 for all these courts. LMA has made available online indexes to the Archdeaconry Court of Middlesex and the Consistory Court of London (from which a scan may be ordered). David Wright has compiled an index to all the London Courts (excluding PCC) for the period 1750-1858. The first part of this has been published as The London Probate Index, surnames A-E:wills & administrations for all courts & peculiars (except the PCC) in London & Middlesex 1750-1858 on CD-ROM. The compiler will undertake to search the remainder of the index for a fee and details can be found in Gibson's guide.

However, until these initiatives are completed, and for the later and earlier periods, the contemporary calendars must be used, except for the Archdeaconry Court of London, where an index has been published by the Society of Genealogists to the post-1700 wills (and the index is available online at Origins). These works are all more fully listed in Gibson's work, together with details of the more minor courts.

Again, the London researcher can only be encouraged to search all these indexes and courts, and look at any will of a person of his names of interest, unless that name is very common. Wills are not merely the most personal of documents to have been handed down to us. Occasionally, (and it is commoner with London testators than any others), the testator leaves a bequest to a country parish church, especially before about 1700, or in some other way indicates a link which might never otherwise be suspected. Even when the bequest does not take the form of 'to the parish of Littletown where I was born', this can frequently be inferred and confirmed from other evidence.

Letters of Administration (often referred to by the abbreviation 'Admons' or 'Adcons') were issued to people who undertook to distribute the goods of a deceased person properly. They were most often granted when a person died intestate, or when there was some doubt as to the validity of the will, or when the executor had died, was a minor, had failed to prove the will in reasonable time, etc. Several successive administrations could be issued if administrators died before an estate was completely wound up. In extreme cases, over a hundred years could pass between a death and the final administration, and in these cases, a family tree over that period may be built up from administrations alone. In general, however, administrations are not as important to the genealogist as are wills, and they certainly do not have the personal flavour a testator can impart.

Where they survive, inventories provide an invaluable list of the possessions of ancestors. They survive in some profusion in the records of the Archdeaconry of Middlesex and to a lesser extent (but largely only to the mid-eighteenth century) in the PCC, but are sparse in the other London courts. An index to inventories in the Deanery of St Paul's is available online at **www.history.ac.uk/gh/**. Where a will was disputed the most wonderful detail can emerge, and long genealogical charts are not uncommon[44].

The London researcher (of an uncommon name at least) need not and should not restrict his wills research to the London courts. Rural testators quite frequently left bequests to children, grandchildren, nephews, etc. in London and stated that that was where they were, often with a specific parish and/or trade to assist identification. Furthermore, well-off London merchants would frequently retire to country estates, and have their wills proved in the local probate court.

CHAPTER NINE
Apprenticeship, livery company and occupational records

The vast array of apprenticeship and livery company (or guild) records are a unique source for London genealogy. Other cities may have records for a guild or two – London has records of getting on for a hundred. Until quite modern times, nobody could work in the City unless they were a member of a livery company or apprenticed to someone who was. This was one of the reasons for the growth of the suburbs. While this was more and more frequently ignored after about 1750, it remained an important factor until the beginning of the nineteenth century.

Some of the older and larger livery companies retain their own records, but the vast majority of the companies have deposited their older records in the Guildhall Library. Even with the move of most Guildhall Library records to LMA, these records remain at Guildhall. In addition, the City kept a central record and index of freedom admissions, which unfortunately only survives from the late 17th century. They were at the Corporation of London Records Office, which has also been amalgamated with LMA. From the latter can be discovered an individual's company, whose records can then be examined.

Very large numbers of rural people apprenticed their children to Londoners. It was an ideal way of providing for those sons who were not going to inherit land, and, in many cases, could lead to great material success. Age at apprenticeship did vary, but was normally between fourteen and sixteen, which can provide a clue when looking for a baptism.

From 1694 London apprenticeships were liable for tax, the proceeds of which were used to maintain orphans. Livery companies were enjoined to keep specific records of apprenticeships for the purposes of collecting the tax, but in practice many of them had done so for 200 years or more before. In addition the court minutes of many companies list all apprenticeships and all list grants of freedom. These records vary in the amount of detail they give. The best (and there are many of these) give the name, parish and occupation of the father of the apprentice. A very large proportion of these (unlike the subject of settlement examinations) disclose a rural origin.

A considerable amount of work has been done to provide indexes to this material, though much remains unindexed. However, provided the individual's company has been established, it should be possible to find the record of his apprenticeship fairly easily, if it survives. The Society of Genealogists is currently publishing a series of indexes to pre-1800 apprenticeships in Livery Company registers, and over 40 volumes have already appeared.

There are many additional livery company records that can provide much more detail about an ancestor once you have identified him. Elderly members could be relieved by the company, and this, or their disappearance from the 'quarterage books' (which are accounts of the membership dues) may give a clue to their date of death. Also, these and other sources may provide addresses, helping you to locate individuals in parochial records. A list of the records at the Guildhall Library has been printed[45].

From 1710, the Inland Revenue raised a tax on apprenticeships. These records are far from comprehensive - they don't, for example, cover pauper apprenticeships, nor those where no premium was payable (usually intra-family apprenticeships). This seems to result in only perhaps one fifth of apprenticeships being taxed and thus recorded. Nonetheless, they are extremely useful as until about 1750 the name and parish of the father are given. Recognising the importance of this material, the Society of Genealogists organised a team of indexers who provided full indexes of masters and apprentices in these records up to 1774. Copies of these indexes on microfilm are available also at the Guildhall Library and through Family History Centres. They are also available online through the Origins website. Not only do these provide overall indexes for this period, but they also contain make reference to apprenticeship to members of companies whose records no longer survive.

Not all masters were members of livery companies and so not all apprenticeships were recorded by them. Apprenticeship indentures may be found, therefore, in parish accumulations, family archives and the like, but this may need a difficult and protracted search without much prospect of success.

Several trades have their own sources, quite apart from livery company records. Of especial use for Londoners are records of mariners. London was always the leading port of England, and the parishes along the banks of the Thames housed large numbers of sailors and those such as shipwrights and chandlers who depended on the marine trade for a living. There are various guides to such records[46]. The Society of Genealogists has published a calendar to the Trinity House Petitions, whereby poor sailors and their families applied for relief to Trinity House. This calendar is rich in material on Londoners. They are available online on the Origins website.

The professions were always centred in London, and again there are special sources for such people as doctors, clergymen and lawyers. The sources for them in the National Archives are described succinctly in Tracing Your Ancestors in the National Archives (A. Bevan, National Archives Handbook 19, 2006) and brief bibliographies are given in A Guide to London and Middlesex Genealogy and Records (C. Webb, West Surrey FHS Research Aids 36, 5th edition, 2005) and Stuart Raymond's Londoners' Occupations: a genealogical guide (FFHS, 2nd edition, 1996).

CHAPTER TEN
School Records

The records of schools can be useful supplements and substitutes to others for the pursuit of genealogical research, and have considerable value for family history purposes in their own right. A list of London School Records is available[47].

Schools were required to keep certain records under various school codes. For example the Elementary School Code, 1903 laid down that all schools should have (a) registers of admission, progress and withdrawal (b) attendance registers and (c) a register of summaries. Other ordinances required that each headmaster should keep a log book. It was specified that records were to be kept for not less than ten years after the last entry had been made in them. Unfortunately, many head teachers over the years have used this regulation, salvage drives and general clear-outs as excuses for wholesale destruction of these invaluable sources, however, mercifully, a very large amount of material remains.

The information to be contained in the records was specified. Entries in admission registers were to be made for each child on entry to the school. Each entry had to contain an individual reference number, date of admission, full name, name and address of parent or guardian, whether exemption from religious education was claimed, date of birth, last school

attended prior to this one, date of leaving school. Secondary school admission registers also usually give any educational attainments such as certificates, and brief details of immediate future career, be it higher education or a job. Most admission registers consist of long lists of entries (sometimes with integral indexes), each entry spreading over a wide double page. Some (especially later) ones, however, are much more lavish with space and have a page for each pupil.

For example, Robert William Cushion, pupil number 276 was admitted to a Fulham infants' school on the 20th March 1905. His father was Robert Cushion of 103 Clonmore Street; he was not exempted from religious instruction. He had been born 7 July 1899, had previously attended Holy Cross School, Fulham, and discharged 25 July 1906 on moving to the junior mixed school.

Admission and discharge registers are a very useful supplement to the Registrar General's records, helping to identify a correct individual from other known information. In an ideal case, it may be possible to trace an individual back from their first job, through a series of schools, and obtaining confirmation of father's name and various addresses which may enable other sources to be tapped. These registers are also included within LMA's contract with Ancestry.com and may be expected to appear in the life of this edition.

Registers overlap and all should be searched for any individual. Often a register covering a period when a school is known by one name has been deposited and allocated a reference denoting a different name. All possible school names need to be researched.

Log books were to be kept up daily with the 'briefest entry to specify the progress of the school or its teachers'. They are generally stout bound plain lined notebooks. Considerable details are given of the comings and goings, shortcomings and illnesses of staff. Rather less appears on individual pupils, though very informative items do occur. All manner of material may be found in log books. Surprising snippets of information appear 'it was very foggy this week, so many pupils absent'; 'Her Majesty Queen Victoria died today; God Save the King'; 'all the desks broken in to and Flower Festival money stolen'. Though not usually as directly genealogically useful as admission and discharge registers, they do give the flavour of the school which a person of interest attended.

Though for most schools, admission and discharge registers and log books are the only records to survive, a wide variety of miscellaneous records may be found more sporadically. The most common miscellaneous items are punishment books. Rather surprisingly, it seems there was no requirement to keep such books until after the

Second World War, and even then, survival is poor. They list the name (and sometimes age) of the pupil, date of punishment and punishment given. In most schools, corporal punishment was the norm, though a few even at an early date had apparently abandoned its use, and detentions, and other non-physical punishments are recorded in the punishment book.

The vast majority of London school records are held at LMA, where such records were deposited for schools closing before 1990. Most there are in the official series of school records, though the records of some parish schools are to be found listed with the parish records. If a school was amalgamated with another school, the successor should have the records or know where they are. Since 1990, however, Borough Archives are receiving new deposits of school records. In any case, Borough Archives should not be neglected, as they are likely to have material of interest to anyone researching a school within their area.

Private schools have generally retained their own records, though a number have deposited their older records at LMA or Borough Archives. Church of England schools records may also be found not only at LMA and the appropriate Borough Archives, but also at the Church of England Records Centre, Galleywall Road, Bermondsey.

All official school records containing personal information at LMA (with insignificant exceptions) are closed for a period of 65 years, apart from admission and discharge registers, which are closed for 30 years. These closure periods date from the last entry in the register in question which may, unfortunately, lengthen the period substantially. Consideration will not be given to breach this closure for genealogical research, though it may be possible for people who need access for legal reasons, such as those wishing to prove their own birth date for pension purposes and for whom other sources have failed. However, all admission and discharge registers at LMA have been filmed and so are readily available on open access there. Periods of closure in Borough Archives vary quite considerably, and must be investigated in each case individually.

CHAPTER ELEVEN
Newspapers

Newspapers are a difficult source, partially because they have been largely unindexed, partially because of their sheer bulk. However, for the period after the mid-nineteenth century, when the local press proliferated, they are an extremely useful source for pure genealogy and a unique source for family history. The whole run of the Times is available on the Gale website: **www.gale.com/Times**. Though this is a pay per view site, many local libraries subscribe to Gale's service and make it freely available to their members. The British Library is digitising a very large proportion of its 19th century newspapers and some 2,000,000 pages have so far been put online. Again, many local councils have made this freely available to their library users.

Before the mid-nineteenth century, newspapers, even local ones, contained mainly national and international news compiled from the London press. A newspaper article may contain almost any information about an ancestor. Obviously, the better-off and more prominent an ancestor was, the more likely you are to discover interesting material about him in newspapers, but even the poor often rated mentions, even if all too often in the columns devoted to criminal activity!

As an example, Richard Garner was mentioned above. He had been clerk to the Board of Works of St Olave Southwark for many years, but had

unfortunately become insane. The local newspaper of the time reported on the meeting of the Board of Works which agreed that he could no longer continue, and provided significant information on him. Unfortunately, it was also clear that some information was omitted from the newspaper reports which would be of great interest to the descendant.

Researchers should always look as a matter of course in the local press to see if the funeral of an ancestor was mentioned, though prior to the 1860s only fairly well-known local figures or those of some notoriety are likely to be mentioned. A funeral notice will often include a large number of the immediate and not-so-immediate family, occasionally indicating a place of origin. It will normally indicate a place of burial, something otherwise very difficult to establish as it does not appear on death certificates. Coroners' records are extremely patchy, and, in any case, for people who died suddenly, whether by accident, misadventure, murder or suicide, the record in the contemporary local newspapers are likely to be more comprehensive and contain more personal (if sometimes gory!) detail than any official records.

For any event with a known date, it is worth researching the local newspapers. There were a large number of 'locals' in every corner of London, and what is not found in one may well be found in another. Reading a year's local newspaper for an area of interest may, by pure luck, give some information of value, but whether it does or not, it will give an insight into the area of interest that no other source can provide.

A simple guide to local newspapers in London and Middlesex is to be found in another guide by Jeremy Gibson[48].

Two sources which are not newspapers in the normal sense, but similar sources are the Gentleman's Magazine and the London Gazette.

The former periodical ran from 1731 to 1908. Until 1861, it printed very large numbers of births, marriages and deaths. While, as you would expect, the upper classes predominate, there are many entries for middle class people, or those with a peculiarity e.g. of longevity and London is very well represented. R.H. Farrar printed an index to Births and Marriages 1731 to 1862 in 1886, and in 1891 the Index Society produced an index to death notices 1731 to 1780. The volumes for 1731-50 have been digitised and are available at **www.bodley.ox.ac.uk/ilej/** .

The London Gazette is one of the official newspapers of record in the United Kingdom. It lists official business such as appointments, medals and awards and the like. Certain legal notices have to be printed in it. The period from 1752 to 1998 has been digitized and is available at **http://www.gazettes-online.co.uk/index.asp?webType=0**.

CHAPTER TWELVE

Manorial and other records of land ownership

Manorial records, by their very nature, are the records of rural areas. However, as already described, the area covered by London has gradually grown, and the area now urbanised includes many manors with extensive records, which even into the nineteenth century can provide useful details of the transmission of land through generations. However, manorial records are not as important in the London area as in more rural ones. Simple guides to manorial records in the ancient counties of Middlesex and Surrey have appeared[49].

A vast number of deeds for London and Middlesex survive in the National Archives (mainly for the medieval period however), in LMA and in the local borough archives. There is no central catalogue of them, and finding the deeds of any given place or property is a matter of considerable luck, as well as usually a lengthy search. However, deeds can give a lot of information, and can occasionally indicate origins, as when a countryman buys a London property.

Middlesex was fortunate in having one of the few central registries of deeds from the early eighteenth century. Its voluminous records from 1709 are deposited at LMA. Deeds 1709-16 have a typescript calendar, but

thereafter the searcher must use annual index volumes, which have been recently published on film. The records of the registry are described in 'The Deeds Registries of Yorkshire and Middlesex' (Journal of the Society of Archivists Vol.6 no.5, 1980).

Much material of this nature survives in family accumulations, business archives and in various collections made by antiquaries. Again, each borough archive has collections of such matter, and there are centrally-deposited items at the British Library Department of Manuscripts, LMA, etc.

In 1873, the government launched an enquiry into the ownership of land in Great Britain, and the results of this enquiry were printed as Parliamentary Papers. These list all people who owned an acre of land or more, giving the owner's name and address, the amount of land owned and the rental value of these lands. The survey unfortunately excluded the metropolis, but is valuable for the area outside. Several counties have been reprinted, including the Middlesex and Surrey sections[50].

CHAPTER THIRTEEN
Criminal and civil legal records

We are fortunate in this country to have documentary sources unrivalled in size and duration, principally as a result of our freedom for nearly a thousand years from invasion, and relative lack of internal strife. Records of criminal cases go back to the early medieval period, but it would be foolish to pretend that they are easy to use in most cases.

Less serious crimes, and many administrative matters, were dealt with in Quarter Sessions. Middlesex Quarter Sessions records are at LMA and a printed guide to them has appeared[51]. Abstracts have appeared in print of the records 1549-1709[52] and following the printed material there is a long series of duplicated calendars down to the mid-eighteenth century at LMA. Surrey Quarter Sessions Records (which included cases in the Metropolitan area south of the Thames) are at the Surrey History Centre, Woking. Again the earliest records have been printed[53], and typescript calendars in the Surrey History Centre continue into the early eighteenth century.

From the thirteenth century to 1971, more serious crimes were dealt with at the Assizes. The records of the Assizes are in the National Archives, Kew. Assize records are divided into circuits, Essex, Kent and Surrey being in the Home Circuit. The early indictments in this circuit have been published[54].

London and Middlesex had 'sessions of oyer and terminer and gaol delivery'; the London and Middlesex records of these are both at LMA, the former in the old Corporation of London Record Office archive. In 1834, this court was replaced by the Central Criminal Court (at the Old Bailey) whose records are in the National Archives. The best source for these, however, is the Old Bailey Sessions Papers of which there is a complete set at the Guildhall Library. Old Bailey Proceedings 1674-1913 are available online at **www.oldbaileyonline.org/** These contain records of some 200,000 trials. This material has been subsumed into another website **http://www.londonlives.org/** which includes an array of additional 18th century material, including poor law and hospital records.

Some important cases were held before the Court of King's Bench which records are also in the National Archives, but there are few finding aids to them. Until 1834, jurisdiction in naval matters (with a large volume of London business) was exercised by the High Court of Admiralty. Again, the records are in the National Archives.

National Archives class HO 26 (for 1791-1849) and HO 27 (for 1850-92) contain registers of criminal trials in more or less chronological order, and can be useful in quickly identifying when a case occurred. The National Archives also has extensive records of prisoners, for details of which the searcher should consult Tracing Your Ancestors in the National Archives and in various leaflets published by the National Archives and available on the Internet. Stuart Tamblin has produced a continuing series of indexes to these records on CD-ROM.

The National Archives holds a vast amount of material concerning civil litigation, on such matters as debts, property rights, inheritance of land, etc. Much of this material contains unique genealogical information. In general, however, it must be said that the earlier the period in which one is interested, the more the National Archives holdings are likely to help you. In the first place this is because such finding aids as there are, are considerably better in general before about the middle of the seventeenth century than after, and, secondly, because it would seem that the ordinary man resorted to the law courts a great deal more, and over much more trivial matters, before about 1650.

Prior to the Civil War, there were a large number of courts exercising civil jurisdiction, such as the Court of Star Chamber and the Court of Requests which were not restored after the Restoration. The great Court of Chancery continued, however, as did its sister court, the Court of the Exchequer. The London Record Society has recently produced an edition[55] of London pleadings in the Exchequer court for two short periods, indicating the wealth of material available in the whole. Finding a case involving your ancestors in the Court of Chancery can be very difficult, but extremely rewarding. Later cases, however, are listed in a very simple manner, under the surname of the first plaintiff. The cases are then listed alphabetically, but not lexicographically. The only other information given is the surname of the first defendant and a reference. With a fairly unusual surname, preferably beginning with an unusual letter, therefore, it is possible to pick out the cases where persons of potential interest were the first plaintiff. It is virtually impossible to list cases where they are defendants, and quite impossible to find cases where they were the second or subsequent plaintiff or defendant, and this situation is unlikely to change quickly, given the huge size of the archive concerned. The best hope is to find a reference in the Bernau index, mentioned above. However, retrospective improvements are being made to the finding aids, and these are being added to the National Archives online catalogue.

The Exchequer cases are simpler to research, since there are printed calendars for much of the period, giving the county in the first column. This enables one to pick out cases of interest a great deal more easily, not least because this court had a much smaller volume of work than Chancery. Again, the High Court of Admiralty had a civil jurisdiction, and has extensive records of interest to London research.

CHAPTER FOURTEEN
Depositions

D epositions in general have been one of the Cinderellas of genealogical research, though their value has long been noted. Depositions are the written record of the answers and/or evidence of witnesses. In the secular courts (whose records are virtually all in the National Archives), the procedure was that 'interrogatories' (i.e. lists of questions) were prepared and then the deponents (i.e. witnesses) were questioned and their answers recorded. Both interrogatories and depositions were then filed, sometimes in separate series, sometimes with the other papers of the court such as the 'bills and answers' (basically the original allegation and first answer of the defendant). In most courts, the records are in English, even before 1733.

Depositions were also taken in ecclesiastical courts, archdeacons', deanery and bishops' courts. The procedure was slightly different in that the records are normally found in books, rather than as loose papers, and there are no interrogatories. Each deposition is headed (in Latin until 1733 apart from the Commonwealth) with the deponent's details, and then his or her evidence.

The information given about the deponent in the heading or introduction to the deposition varies both over time and between ecclesiastical and secular courts. In the secular courts, it was normal to give name, parish, age and

occupation more or less throughout. In the ecclesiastical courts until the first quarter of the eighteenth century, and sometimes thereafter, not only is this information given but also either the birthplace or, in the case of a married woman, the length of time a person had been married. The period of residence in the parish is also frequently given.

The main ecclesiastical court with depositions in London is the Consistory Court of London, with depositions from the 16th to early 19th century at LMA.

The information available from these records is often unique, and it is unfortunate that the only indexes to Consistory Court of London deponents are either to periods after birthplaces cease to be given, or in the case of a printed index to some early records, the calendar[56] does not give the birthplace. However, an index to the 1703-13 period has appeared[57]. For the secular courts we are luckier, in that much of this material (though by no means all) was indexed by Charles Bernau and a team of workers, and appears in his great index.

A microfilm copy of Bernau's Index is at the Society of Genealogists. A guide to this index is available from the Society.

1. Streets, Parishes and Wards in the City of London (C. Webb, West Surrey FHS Research Aids 30, 2005).
2. A to Z of Elizabethan London (A. Prockter and R. Taylor, 1979); A to Z of Restoration London (R. Hyde, 1992); A to Z of Georgian London (R. Hyde, 1981); A to Z of Regency London (P. Laxton, 1985); A to Z of Victorian London (R. Hyde, 1987); Ward Maps of the City of London (R. Hyde, 1999).
3. Poor Law Union Records 1. South-East England and East Anglia (J. Gibson, C. Rogers and C. Webb, FFHS, 2nd ed., 1997).
4. Genealogical Research in Victorian London (C. Webb, West Surrey FHS Research Aids 6, 8th edition, 2005); Genealogical Research in late Victorian and Edwardian London (C. Webb, West Surrey FHS Research Aids 15, 5th edition, 2004).
5. Reproduced on CD-ROM by and available from Archive CD Books.
6. See West Middlesex FHS Magazine 2: 2, Spring 1981.
7. Printed by Hackney Archives Department.
8. Available on CD-ROM (http://www.jenlibrary.u-net.com/disk.htm).
9. Printed by East of London FHS.
10. Printed by Hackney Archives Department.
11. Available on CD-ROM (http://www.jenlibrary.u-net.com/disk.htm).
12. Printed by Hackney Archives Department.
13. A Genealogical Gazetteer of Mid-Victorian London (C. Webb, West Surrey FHS, Research Aids 8, 2000). The parish references used are those in Genealogical Research in Victorian London.
14. Archive CD Books Ireland (http://www.archivecdbooks.ie/).
15. Early 20th Century London: Maps, Street Names And Schools (compiled and indexed by C. Willis, edited by S. Turner, West Surrey FHS CD16, 2009).
16. Old Ordnance Survey Maps Of London - Indexes to the Godfrey Edition (G.C. Dickinson, West Surrey FHS Research Aids 43-47).

17. Atlas and Index of Parish Registers (C. Humphery-Smith, Phillimore, 2nd edition, 1995).
18. A Guide to Middlesex Parish Documents (C. Webb, West Surrey FHS Research Aids 33, 5th edition, 2004).
19. http://www.originsnetwork.com/
20. City of London Burial Index 1813-1853 (West Surrey FHS Microfiche Series 6)
21. Greater London Cemeteries and Crematoria (comp. P.S.Wolfston, revised by C. Webb, Society of Genealogists, 6th edition, 2006).
22. Bishops' Transcripts and Marriage Licences, Bonds and Allegations (J. Gibson, FFHS, 5th edition, 2001).
23. Kent (Volume 4, 1980); Surrey (Volume 4 Part 1, 1990); Essex (Volume 9 Part 4, 1993); London and Middlesex (Volume 9 Part 5, 2nd ed., 2002); Hertfordshire (Volume 9 Part 6, 1999).
24. The Allegations for Marriage Licences issued by the Commissary Court of Surrey between 1673-1770 (A.R. Bax, 1906-1907).
25. Commissary Court of Surrey Allegations for Marriage Licences 1662-1665; 1674-1770 (West Surrey FHS Microfiche Series 26).
26. Catholic Missions and Registers 1700-1880 Volume 1 London and the Home Counties (M. Gandy, 1993).
27. Irregular Marriage in London before 1754 (T. Benton, Society of Genealogists, 1993).
28. A List of Middlesex Monumental Inscriptions (C. Webb, West Surrey FHS Research Aids 48, 2005).
29. The Monumental Inscriptions of Surrey: a list of copies (T. Wilcock, West Surrey FHS Research Aids 19, 2nd edition, 1991).
30. Churchwardens' Accounts of Parishes within the City of London (Guildhall Library, 2nd edition, 1969); Vestry Minutes of Parishes within the City of London (Guildhall Library, 2nd edition, 1964); London Rate Assessments and Inhabitants' Lists (Guildhall Library, 2nd edition, 1968).
31. A Guide to Middlesex Parish Documents (C. Webb, West Surrey FHS Research Aids 33, 5th ed., 2004); A Provisional List of City of London Poor Law Records (C. Webb, West Surrey FHS Research Aids 28, 2nd edition, 1992).
32. Londoners' Occupations: a genealogical guide (S.A. Raymond, FFHS, 1994)
33. The Directories of London (P.J. Atkins, 1991).
34. Middlesex Directories - A Finding List (C. Webb, West Surrey FHS Research Aids 37, 2nd edition, 1998); Surrey Directories - A Finding List (C. Webb, West Surrey FHS Research Aids 29, 2nd edition, 1994).
35. Poll Books c1696-1872: A Directory to Holdings in Great Britain (J. Gibson and C. Rogers, FFHS, 3rd edition, 1994).
36. Electoral Registers since 1832; and Burgess Rolls (J. Gibson and C. Rogers, FFHS, 2nd edition, 1990).

37. An Index to the Association Oath Rolls for the City of London (C. Webb, West Surrey FHS RS40, 2006).
38. London and Middlesex A Genealogical Bibliography (S. A. Raymond, FFHS, 2nd edition, 1998) covers printed sources. Lists of Londoners (J. Gibson and H. Creaton (FFHS, 1994) lists unpublished indexes to such material. A Guide to London & Middlesex Genealogy and Records (C. Webb, West Surrey FHS Research Aids 36, 5th ed., 2005) provides a brief encyclopaedic guide arranged by subjects. A List of Books and Articles about London and Middlesex Place (C. Webb, West Surrey FHS Research Aids 39, 3rd ed., 2006) lists printed histories and other material by parish.
39. A Guide to Middlesex Parish Documents including Poor Law Records (C. Webb, West Surrey FHS Research Aids 33, 2004).
40. City Settlement Examinations Vol. 1: St Botolph Aldgate 1742-1868 (C. Webb, WSFHS RS 41, 2007).
41. 'Post-1834 Poor Law Records' (C.R. Webb, *Genealogists' Magazine* 19: 3, September 1977).
42. An Index to the Wills Proved in the Prerogative Court of Canterbury 1750-1800 (A.J. Camp, Society of Genealogists, 1976-92).
43. Probate Jurisdictions: where to look for wills (J. Gibson, FFHS, 6th ed., 2002).
44. See Wills, Inventories and Death Duties: a Provisional Guide (J. Cox, National Archives, 1988).
45. City Livery Companies and Related Organisations (Guildhall Library Research Guide 3, 3rd ed., 1989).
46. e.g., Naval Records for Genealogists (N.A.M. Rodger, National Archives Handbook 22, 1988).
47. An Index of London Schools and their Records (C. Webb, SoG, 3rd ed., 2007).
48. Local Newspapers 1750-1920 (Jeremy Gibson, FFHS, 1987).
49. A Guide to London & Middlesex Manorial Records (C. Webb, West Surrey West Surrey FHS Research Aids 38, 2006); A Guide to Surrey Manorial Records (C. Webb, West Surrey FHS Research Aids 35, 2nd ed., 2005).
50. The Return of Owners of Land 1873: Surrey (West Surrey Family History Society Record Series 10, 1989); The Return of Owners of Land 1873: Middlesex (West Surrey Family History Society Record Series 13, 1991).
51. Guide to the Middlesex Sessions Records (GLRO, 1965). A simpler guide appears in Quarter Sessions Records for Family Historians (J. Gibson, FFHS, 1983).
52. Middlesex County Records [abstracts 1549-1688] (ed. J.C. Jeaffreson, 1886-92). Calendar of Sessions Records 1612-18 (ed. W. Le Hardy, 1935-41). Calendar of Sessions Books 1689-1709 (ed. W.J. Hardy, 1905).
53. Surrey Records: Sessions Order Books and Rolls 1659-68 (4 vols., ed. D.L. Powell, Surrey Record Society and Surrey County Council, 1934-51).
54. Calendar of Assize Records, Home Circuit Indictments, Elizabeth and James I (J.S. Cockburn, HMSO, 1975-85).

55. Exchequer Equity Pleadings 1685-6 and 1784-5 (ed. H. Horwitz, London Record Society 35, 2000).

56. London Consistory Court Depositions, 1586-1611: List and Indexes (ed. L.L. Giese, London Record Society 32, 1997 for 1995).

57. London's Bawdy Courts Volume I 1703-1713 (ed. C. Webb, SoG, 1999).

APPENDIX 1
London record repositories

Times of openings for all libraries and record offices are subject to change, and a telephone call in advance of a visit is always advisable and sometimes essential.

The National Archives
Ruskin Avenue, Kew, Richmond, TW9 4DU.
Tel: 020 8876 3444 ◆ Email: enquiry@nationalarchives.gov.uk
Website: **www.nationalarchives.gov.uk**
Holds nonconformist registers deposited at various times. Copies at Family Records Society above.

London Metropolitan Archives
40 Northampton Road, London EC1R 0HB.
9.30 am to 7.30 pm Tuesday and Thursday (advance booking necessary for original documents), 9.30 am to 4.45 Monday, Wednesday, Friday. The office is open certain Saturdays. Prospective searchers should check before visiting.
Tel: 020 7332 3820 ◆ Email: ask.lma@corpoflondon.gov.uk
Website: **www.cityoflondon.gov.uk/lma**
This office holds the vast majority of London and Middlesex parish records, outside the Cities of London and Westminster.

St Bartholomew's Hospital Archives and Museum
North Wing, St Bartholomew's Hospital, West Smithfield, London, EC1A 7BE.
Tel: 020 7601 8152 ◆ Email: barts.archives@bartsandthelondon.nhs.uk
Website: **www.brlcf.org.uk**
Holds records of St Bartholomew the Less.

Guildhall Library
Aldermanbury, London EC2P 2EJ.
9.30 am to 4.45 pm Monday to Saturday
Tel: 020 7260 1683 ◆ Fax: 020 7600 3384
Email: manuscripts.guildhall@corpoflondon.gov.uk
Website: **www.history.ac.uk/gh/**
This library holds the archives of most of the City Livery Companies, Lloyd's of London, the Stock Exchange, Christ's Hospital and the records of the Dean and Chapter of St Paul's. Much other material formerly held there is now normally viewed at LMA.

City of Westminster Archives Centre
10 St Ann's Street, London SW1P 2XR.
Tel: 020 7798 2180 ◆ Fax: 020 7641 5179 ◆ Email: archives@westminster.gov.uk
Website: **www.westminster.gov.uk/archives/index.cfm**
9.30 am to 7 pm Monday to Friday, 9.30 am to 5 pm Saturday. This holds most of the registers of parishes within the City of Westminster.

Greenwich Heritage Centre
Artillery Square, Royal Arsenal, SE18 4DX.
Tel: 020 8854 2452 ◆ Email: heritage.centre@greenwich.gov.uk
Website: **www.greenwich.gov.uk/**
9 am to 5.30 pm Monday and Tuesday, 9 am to 8 pm Thursday, 9 am to 5 pm Saturday. This holds the registers of Charlton and some of Greenwich.

Hammersmith and Fulham Archives and Local History Centre
The Lilla Huset, 191 Talgarth Road, London W6 8BJ.
9.30 am to 8 pm Monday, 9.30 am to 1 pm Tuesday, Thursday and first Saturday in the month (advance booking essential for all visits)
Tel: 020 8741 5159 ◆ Email: archives@lbhf.gov.uk
Website: **www.lbhf.gov.uk**
This holds the registers of St Paul, Hammersmith.

Hounslow - Local Studies Collection (Brentford and Chiswick areas)
(a) Chiswick Public Library, Duke's Avenue, Chiswick, London W4 2AB.
Tel: 020 8994 1008
(b) Hounslow Library, Centre Space, Treaty Centre, High Street, Hounslow TW3 1ES.
Tel: 0845 456 2800
Holds Isleworth and East Bedfont registers.
Website: **www.hounslow.gov.uk/libraries**

Lewisham Local Studies and Archives
199 Lewisham High Street, London, SE13 6LG.
Tel: 020 8297 0682 ✦ Email: local.studies@lewisham.gov.uk
Website: **www.lewisham.gov.uk/**
9.30 am to 1 pm, 2 pm to 5 pm Monday and Thursday, 9.30 am to 1 pm, 2 pm to 8 pm Tuesday. This holds the registers of Lee and some of Deptford St Paul and Lewisham.

The following libraries and archives hold no parish register material, but many other archives and local history material. Their hours tend to vary somewhat rapidly and occasionally unpredictably, so a telephone call first is essential.

Barnet Local Studies & Archives Centre
80 Daws Lane, Mill Hill, London NW7 4SL.
Tel: 020 8959 6657 ✦ Email: library.archives@barnet.gov.uk
Website: **www.barnet.gov.uk/index/leisure-culture/libraries**

Bexley Local Studies and Archives Centre
Central Library, Townley Road, Bexleyheath, Kent DA6 7HJ.
Tel: 020 8303 7777 X 3470 ✦ Email: archives@bexley.gov.uk
Website: **www.bexley.gov.uk/service/lib-central.html**

Brent Archive
Willesden Green Library Centre, 95 High Road, Willesden Green NW10 2SF.
Tel: 020 8937 3541 ✦ Email: archives@brent.gov.uk
Website: **www.brent.gov.uk/heritage.nsf**

Bromley Archives and Local Studies Library
Central Library, High Street, Bromley, Kent BR1 1EX.
Tel: 020 8461 7170 ✦ Email: localstudies.library@bromley.gov.uk.
Website: **www.bromley.gov.uk/libraries/librariesintheborough/bromley_archives.htm**

Camden Local Studies and Archives Centre
32-38 Theobalds Road, London WC1X 8PA.
Tel: 020 7974 6342 ✦ Email: localstudies@camden.gov.uk
Website: **www.camden.gov.uk/localstudies**

Croydon Local Studies Library and Archives
Level 3, Central Library, Croydon Clocktower, Katharine Street, Croydon CR9 1ET.
Tel: 020 8760 5400 X 1112 ✦ Email: localstudies@croydon.gov.uk
Website: **www.croydonline.org/history/places/lslibrary.asp**

Ealing Local History Centre
103 Ealing Broadway Centre (first floor), Ealing W5 5JY.
Tel: 020 8825 8194 ♦ Email: joates@ealing.gov.uk
Website: **www.ealing.gov.uk/services/leisure/libraries/local_history_centre/**

Enfield Local History Unit
First Floor, Thomas Hardy House, 39 London Road, Enfield EN2 6DS.
Tel: 020 8379 2724 ♦ Email: local.history@enfield.gov.uk
Website: **www.enfield.gov.uk/Leisure**

Hackney Archives Department
43 De Beauvoir Road, London N1 5SQ.
Tel: 020 7241 2886 ♦ Email: archives@hackney.gov.uk
Website: **www.hackney.gov.uk/ca-archives**

Haringey Archives Department
Bruce Castle, Lordship Lane, London N17 8NU.
Tel: 020 8808 8772 ♦ Email: museum.services@haringey.gov.uk
Website: **www.haringey.gov.uk/leisure/brucecastlemuseum.htm**

Harrow Local History Collection
Civic Centre Library, PO Box 4, Civic Centre, Harrow HA1 2UU.
Tel: 020 8424 1056 ♦ Email: localhistory.library@harrow.gov.uk
Website: **www.harrow.gov.uk/ccm/content/leisure-and-culture/libraries/**

Havering Local Studies Librarian
Central Library, St Edward's Way, Romford, Essex RM1 3AR.
Tel: 01708 432393/4 ♦ Email: Simon.Donoghue@havering.gov.uk
Website: **www.havering.gov.uk**

Hillingdon Local Heritage Service
Central Library, High Street, Uxbridge UB8 1HD.
Tel: 01895 250702 ♦ Email: archives@hillingdongrid.org
Website: **www.hillingdon.gov.uk/libraries/heritage/lsteam.php**

Islington Local History Centre
45 St John Street, London EC1V 4NB.
Tel: 020 7527 7988 ♦ Email: local.history@islington.gov.uk
Website: **www.islington.gov.uk/Education/LocalHistory/localhistorycentre/**

Kensington and Chelsea Local Studies Department
Phillimore Walk, London W8 7RX.
Tel: 020 7361 3010 ◆ Email: information.services@rbkc.gov.uk
Website: **www.rbkc.gov.uk/libraries/**

Lambeth Archives
Minet Library, 52 Knatchbull Road, London SE5 9QY
Tel: 020 7926 6076 ◆ Email: archives@lambeth.gov.uk
Website: **www.lambeth.gov.uk/**

Merton Local Studies Centre
Merton Civic Centre, London Road, Morden SM4 5DX.
Tel: 020 8545 3239 ◆ Email: local.studies@merton.gov.uk
Website: **www.merton.gov.uk/libraries/localstudies.asp**

Newham Archives and Local Studies Library
Stratford Library, 3 The Grove, London E15 1EL.
Tel: 020 8430 6881 ◆ Email: richard.durack@newham.gov.uk
Website: **www.newham.gov.uk/Services/ArchivesAndLocalStudiesLibrary**

Redbridge Local Studies and Archives
Central Library, Clements Road, Ilford, Essex IG1 1EA.
Tel: 020 8708 2414 ◆ Email: local.studies@redbridge.gov.uk
Website: **www.redbridge.gov.uk/learning/localstudies.cfm**

Richmond Local Studies Library
Old Town Hall, Whittaker Avenue, Richmond, Surrey TW9 1TP.
Tel: 020 8332 6820 ◆ Email: localstudies@richmond.gov.uk
Website: **www.richmond.gov.uk/home/leisure_and_culture**

Southwark Local Studies Library
211 Borough High Street, Southwark, London SE1 1JA.
Tel: 020 7525 2000 ◆ Email: local.studies.library@southwark.gov.uk
Website: **www.southwark.gov.uk/DiscoverSouthwark/LocalStudiesLibrary/**

Sutton Archives and Local Studies
2nd Floor, Central Library, St Nicholas Way, Sutton, Surrey SM1 1EA
Tel: 020 8770 4745 ◆ Email: local.studies@sutton.gov.uk
Website: **www.sutton.gov.uk/leisure/heritage/localstudy.htm**

Tower Hamlets History Library and Archives
Bancroft Library, 277 Bancroft Road, London E1 4DQ.
Tel: 020 7364 1290 (history) ♦ Tel: 020 7364 1289 (archives)
Email: localhistory@towerhamlets.gov.uk
Website: **www.towerhamlets.gov.uk**

Waltham Forest Archives
Vestry House Museum, Vestry Road, Walthamstow, London E17 9NH.
Tel: 020 8509 1917 ♦ Email: vestry.house@walthamforest.gov.uk

Wandsworth Local History Service
Battersea Library, 265 Lavender Hill, London SW11 1JB.
Tel: 020 8871 7753 ♦ Email: localhistory@wandsworth.gov.uk
Website: **www.wandsworth.gov.uk/**

APPENDIX 2
Parishes in Greater London

This provides an alphabetical listing of ancient parishes in the Greater London area, their original county, hundred, registration district, metropolitan borough if appropriate, London borough, probate jurisdiction, family history society. The City of London is excluded. The following abbreviations are used:

Archd.Ess = Archdeaconry of Essex; Archd.Lnd = Archdeaconry of London; Archd.Mdx = Archdeaconry of Middlesex; Archd.Roc = Archdeaconry of Rochester; Comm.Lnd = Commissary Court of London; Croydon = Peculiar Deanery of Croydon; E.Lnd = East of London Family History Society; E.Sry = East Surrey Family History Society. It should be noted that East and West Surrey Family History Societies cooperate on research matters, so that West Surrey Family History Society holds much research material for the whole county, especially with regard to register transcripts, census indexes and probate material; Herts = Hertfordshire; n/a = not applicable; N.Mdx = London Westminster and North Middlesex Family History Society; NW.Kent = North West Kent Family History Society; St Kath. = Peculiar of St Katharine by the Tower; St Paul's = Peculiar of the Dean and Chapter of St Paul's; Shore = Peculiar Deanery of Shoreham; Sry = Surrey probate courts; Sry/Lnd = Surrey probate courts until 1845, London 1845-58; Waltham = Waltham Forest Family History Society; W.Mdx = West Middlesex Family History Society; W.Mdx/Hill = West Middlesex Family History Society and Hillingdon Family History Society; W'min = Peculiar of the Dean and Chapter of Westminster; Woolw. = Woolwich and District Family History Society

Parish	County	Hundred	Reg. Dist.	Metro. Borough	London Borough	Probate	FHS
Acton	Middlesex	Ossulstone	Brentford	n/a	Ealing	Comm.Lnd	W.Mdx
Addington	Surrey	Wallington	Croydon	n/a	Croydon	Sry	E.Sry
Ashford[1]	Middlesex	Spelthorne	Staines	n/a	n/a	Archd.Mdx	W.Mdx
Barking	Essex	Becontree	Romford	n/a	Barking	Archd.Ess	E.Lnd
Barnes	Surrey	Brixton	Richmond	n/a	Richmond	Croydon	E.Sry
Battersea	Surrey	Brixton	Wandsworth	Battersea	Wandsworth	Sry/Lnd	E.Sry
Beckenham	Kent	Bromley	Bromley	n/a	Bromley	Archd.Roc	NW.Kent
Beddington	Surrey	Wallington	Croydon	n/a	Sutton	Sry	E.Sry
Bermondsey	Surrey	Brixton	Bermondsey[2]	Bermondsey	Southwark	Sry/Lnd	E.Sry
Bethnal Green	Middlesex	Ossulstone	Bethnal Grn	Bethnal Green	Tower Hamlets	Comm.Lnd	E.Lnd
Bexley	Kent	Ruxley	Dartford	n/a	Bexley	Shore	NW.Kent
Bloomsbury	Middlesex	Ossulstone	St Giles	Holborn	Camden	Comm.Lnd	N.Mdx
Brentford (New)[3]	Middlesex	Elthorne	Brentford	n/a	Hounslow	Archd.Mdx	W.Mdx
Bromley	Kent	Bromley	Bromley	n/a	Bromley	Archd.Roc	NW.Kent
Bromley by Bow[4]	Middlesex	Ossulstone	Poplar	Poplar	Tower Hamlets	Comm.Lnd	E.Lnd
Camberwell	Surrey	Brixton	Camberwell	Camberwell	Southwark	Sry/Lnd	E.Sry
Carshalton	Surrey.	Wallington	Epsom	n/a	Sutton	Sry	E.Sry
Charlton	Kent	Blackheath[5]	Lewisham	Greenwich	Greenwich	Archd.Roc	NW.Kent/ Woolw.
Cheam	Surrey	Wallington	Epsom	n/a	Sutton	Croydon	E.Sry
Chelsea	Middlesex	Ossulstone	Chelsea	Chelsea	Kens/Chelsea	Archd.Mdx	W.Mdx
Chelsfield	Kent	Ruxley	Bromley	n/a	Bromley	Archd.Roc	NW.Kent
Chelsham	Surrey	Tandridge	Godstone	n/a	Croydon	Sry	E.Sry
Chessington	Surrey	Kingston	Epsom	n/a	Kingston	Sry	E.Sry
Chigwell[6]	Essex	Ongar	Epping	n/a	Redbridge	Archd.Ess	E.Lnd
Chingford	Essex	Waltham	Epping	n/a	Waltham Forest	Comm.Lnd	Waltham
Chislehurst	Kent	7	Bromley	n/a	Bromley	Archd.Roc	NW.Kent
Chiswick	Middlesex	Ossulstone	Brentford	n/a	Hounslow	St Paul's	W.Mdx

74

	Surrey	Brixton	Wandsworth	Wandsworth	Wandsworth	Sry/Lnd	E.Sry
Clapham							
Clerkenwell							
St James	Middlesex	Ossulstone	Holborn	Finsbury	Camden	Archd.Lnd	N.Mdx
St John	Middlesex	Ossulstone	Holborn	Finsbury	Camden	Archd.Lnd	N.Mdx
Coulsdon	Surrey	Wallington	Croydon	n/a	Croydon	Sry	E.Sry
Covent Garden	Middlesex	Westminster	Strand	Westminster	Westminster	Archd.Mdx	N.Mdx
Cowley	Middlesex	Elthorne	Uxbridge	n/a	Hillingdon	Archd.Mdx	W.Mdx/ Hill
Cranford	Middlesex	Elthorne	Staines	n/a	Hounslow	Archd.Mdx	W.Mdx
Cranham	Essex	Chafford	Romford	n/a	Havering	Archd.Ess	E.Lnd
Crayford	Kent	Lessness	Dartford	n/a	Bexley	Shore	NW.Kent
Croydon	Surrey	Wallington	Croydon	n/a	Croydon	Croydon	E.Sry
Cudham	Kent	Ruxley	Bromley	n/a	Bromley	Archd.Roc	NW.Kent
Dagenham	Essex	Becontree	Romford	n/a	Barking	Archd.Ess	E.Lnd
Deptford[8]							
St Nicholas	Kent	Greenwich	Greenwich	Greenwich	Lewisham	Archd.Roc	NW.Kent
St Paul	Kent/Surrey	Brixton	Greenwich	Greenwich	Lewisham	Archd.Roc	NW.Kent
Downe	Kent	Ruxley	Bromley	n/a	Bromley	Shore	NW.Kent
Ealing	Middlesex	Ossulstone	Brentford	n/a	Ealing	Comm.Lnd	W.Mdx
East Barnet N.Mdx/Herts	Herts	Cashio	Barnet	n/a	Barnet	Herts	
East Bedfont	Middlesex	Spelthorne	Staines	n/a	Hounslow	Archd.Mdx	W.Mdx
East Ham	Essex	Becontree	West Ham	n/a	Newham	Archd.Ess	E.Lnd
East Wickham	Kent	Lessness	Dartford	n/a	Bexley	Shore	NW.Kent
Edgware	Middlesex	Gore	Hendon	n/a	Barnet	Comm.Lnd	N.Mdx
Edmonton	Middlesex	Edmonton	Edmonton	n/a	Enfield	Comm.Lnd	N.Mdx
Eltham	Kent	Blackheath	Lewisham	Woolwich	Greenwich	Archd.Roc	NW.Kent
Enfield	Middlesex	Edmonton	Edmonton	n/a	Enfield	Comm.Lnd	N.Mdx
Erith	Kent	Lessness	Dartford	n/a	Bexley	Archd.Roc	NW.Kent

Parish	County	Hundred	Reg. Dist.	Metro. Borough	London Borough	Probate	FHS
Farleigh	Surrey	Tandridge	Godstone	n/a	Croydon	Sry	E.Sry
Farnborough	Kent	Ruxley	Bromley	n/a	Bromley	Archd.Roc	NW.Kent
Feltham[1]	Middlesex	Spelthorne	Staines	n/a	Hounslow	Archd.Mdx	W.Mdx
Finchley	Middlesex	Ossulstone	Barnet	n/a	Barnet	Comm.Lnd	N.Mdx
Foots Cray[9]	Kent	Ruxley	Bromley	n/a	Bromley	Archd.Roc	NW.Kent
Friern Barnet	Middlesex	Ossulstone	Barnet	n/a	Barnet	St Paul's	N.Mdx
Fulham	Middlesex	Ossulstone	Fulham	Fulham	Hammersmith	Comm.Lnd	W.Mdx
Great Ilford	Essex	Becontree	Romford	n/a	Redbridge	Archd.Ess	E.Lnd
Great Stanmore	Middlesex	Gore	Hendon	n/a	Harrow	Comm.Lnd	N.Mdx
Great Warley	Essex	Chafford	Romford	n/a	Havering	Archd.Ess	E.Lnd
Greenford[10]	Middlesex	Elthorne	Brentford	n/a	Ealing	Comm.Lnd	W.Mdx
Greenwich[11]	Kent	Blackheath	Greenwich	Greenwich	Greenwich	Archd.Roc	NW.Kent
Hackney	Middlesex	Ossulstone	Hackney	Hackney	Hackney	Comm.Lnd	E.Lnd
Hammersmith	Middlesex	Ossulstone	Kensington	Hemmersmith	Hammersmith	Comm.Lnd	W.Mdx
Hampstead[12]	Middlesex	Ossulstone	Hampstead[13]	Hampstead	Camden	Comm.Lnd	N.Mdx
Hampton	Middlesex	Spelthorne	Kingston	n/a	Richmond	Archd.Mdx	W.Mdx
Hanwell	Middlesex	Elthorne	Brentford	n/a	Ealing	Archd.Mdx	W.Mdx
Hanworth	Middlesex	Spelthorne	Staines	n/a	Hounslow	Comm.Lnd	W.Mdx
Harefield	Middlesex	Elthorne	Uxbridge	n/a	Hillingdon	Comm.Lnd	W.Mdx/Hill
Harlington W.Mdx/Hill	Middlesex	Elthorne	Staines	n/a	Hillingdon	Archd.Mdx	
Harmondsworth	Middlesex	Elthorne	Staines	n/a	Hillingdon	Archd.Mdx	W.Mdx/Hill
Harrow	Middlesex	Gore	Hendon	n/a	Harrow/Brent	Croydon	N.Mdx
Hayes	Kent	Ruxley	Bromley	n/a	Bromley	Shore	NW.Kent
Hayes	Middlesex	Elthorne	Uxbridge	n/a	Hillingdon	Croydon	W.Mdx/Hill

Hendon	Middlesex	Gore	Hendon	n/a	Barnet	Comm.Lnd	N.Mdx
Heston	Middlesex	Isleworth	Brentford	n/a	Hounslow	Archd.Mdx	W.Mdx
Hillingdon	Middlesex	Elthorne	Uxbridge	n/a	Hillingdon	Archd.Mdx	W.Mdx/ Hill
Holborn[14]	Middlesex	Ossulstone	Holborn	Holborn	Camden	Archd.Lnd	N.Mdx
Hornchurch	Essex	Romford	n/a	Havering		Archd.Ess	E.Lnd
Liberty of Havering-atte-Bower							
Hornsey[15]	Middlesex	Ossulstone	Edmonton	n/a	Haringey	Comm.Lnd	N.Mdx
Ickenham	Middlesex	Elthorne	Uxbridge	n/a	Hillingdon	Comm.Lnd	W.Mdx/ Hill
Isleworth	Middlesex	Isleworth	Brentford	n/a	Hounslow	Archd.Mdx	W.Mdx
Islington	Middlesex	Ossulstone	Islington	Islington	Islington	Comm.Lnd	N.Mdx
Kensington	Middlesex	Ossulstone	Kensington	Kensington	Kens./Chelsea	Archd.Mdx	W.Mdx
Keston	Kent	Ruxley	Bromley	n/a	Bromley	Shore	NW.Kent
Kew	Surrey	Kingston	Richmond	n/a	Richmond	Sry	E.Sry
Kingsbury	Middlesex	Gore	Hendon	n/a	Brent	Comm.Lnd	N.Mdx
Kingston	Surrey	Kingston	Kingston	n/a	Kingston	Sry	E.Sry
Knockholt	Kent	Ruxley	Bromley	n/a	Bromley	Archd.Roc	NW.Kent
Laleham[1]	Middlesex	Spelthorne	Staines	n/a	n/a	Archd.Mdx	W.Mdx
Lambeth	Surrey	Brixton	Lambeth	Lambeth	Lambeth	Sry/Lnd	E.Sry
Lee	Kent	Blackheath	Lewisham	Lewisham	Lewisham	Archd.Roc	NW.Kent
Lewisham	Kent	Blackheath	Lewisham	Lewisham	Lewisham	Archd.Roc	NW.Kent
Leyton	Essex	Becontree	West Ham	n/a	Waltham Forest	Comm.Lnd	Waltham
Limehouse	Middlesex	Ossulstone	Stepney	Stepney	Tower Hamlets	Comm.Lnd	E.Lnd
Little Ilford	Essex	Becontree	West Ham	n/a	Newham	Archd.Ess	E.Lnd
Little Stanmore[16]	Middlesex	Gore	Hendon	n/a	Harrow	Comm.Lnd	N.Mdx
Littleton[1]	Middlesex	Spelthorne	Staines	n/a	n/a	Archd.Mdx	W.Mdx
Malden[17]	Surrey	Kingston	Kingston	n/a	Kingston	Sry	E.Sry
Merton	Surrey	Brixton	Croydon	n/a	Merton	Sry	E.Sry

Parish	County	Hundred	Reg. Dist.	Metro. Borough	London Borough	Probate	FHS
Minories	Middlesex	Ossulstone	Whitechapel	Stepney	Tower Hamlets	Archd.Lnd	E.Lnd
Mitcham	Surrey	Wallington	Croydon	n/a	Merton	Sry	E.Sry
Monken Hadley	Middlesex	Edmonton	Barnet	n/a	Barnet	Comm.Lnd	N.Mdx
Morden	Surrey	Wallington	Croydon	n/a	Merton	Sry	E.Sry
Mortlake	Surrey	Brixton	Richmond	n/a	Richmond	Croydon	E.Sry
Newington[18]	Surrey	Brixton	Newington[19]	Southwark	Southwark	Sry/Lnd	E.Sry
North Cray	Kent	Ruxley	Bromley	n/a	Bromley	Archd.Roc	NW.Kent
Northolt	Middlesex	Elthorne	Uxbridge	n/a	Ealing	Comm.Lnd	W.Mdx
Norwood[20]	Middlesex	Elthorne	Uxbridge	n/a	Ealing	Croydon	W.Mdx
Orpington	Kent	Ruxley	Bromley	n/a	Bromley	Shore	NW.Kent
Paddington	Middlesex	Ossulstone	Paddington	Paddington	Westminster	Archd.Mdx/W'min	N.Mdx
Perivale[21]	Middlesex	Elthorne	Brentford	n/a	Ealing	Archd.Lnd	W.Mdx
Petersham	Surrey	Kingston	Richmond	n/a	Richmond	Sry	E.Sry
Pinner	Middlesex	Gore	Hendon	n/a	Harrow	Croydon	N.Mdx
Plumstead	Kent	Lessness	Lewisham[22]	Woolwich	Greenwich	Archd.Roc	NW.Kent/Woolw.
Poplar	Middlesex	Ossulstone	Poplar	Poplar	Tower Hamlets	Comm.Lnd	E.Lnd
Putney	Surrey	Brixton	Wandsworth	Wandsworth	Wandsworth	Croydon	E.Sry
Rainham	Essex	Chafford	Romford	n/a	Havering	Archd.Ess	E.Lnd
Richmond	Surrey	Kingston	Richmond	n/a	Richmond	Sry	E.Sry
Romford	Essex	Romford	n/a		Havering	Archd.Ess	E.Lnd
Rotherhithe	Surrey	Brixton	Rotherhithe[23]	Bermondsey	Southwark	Sry/Lnd	E.Sry
Ruislip	Middlesex	Elthorne	Uxbridge	n/a	Hillingdon	Comm.Lnd	W.Mdx/Hill
St Bot.Aldgate	Middlesex	Ossulstone	Whitechapel	Stepney	Tower Hamlets	Archd.Lnd	E.Lnd
St Clement Danes	Middlesex	Westminster[24]	Strand	Westminster	Westminster	Archd.Mdx	N.Mdx
St George Han.Sq.	Middlesex	Westminster	St George H.S.	Westminster	Westminster	Archd.Mdx	N.Mdx

Parish	County	Division	District	Sub-district	Borough	Court	Region
St George Martyr	Middlesex	Ossulstone	Holborn	Holborn	Camden	Archd.Lnd	N.Mdx
St George/East	Middlesex	Ossulstone	St George/ East Stepney	St George/ East Stepney	Tower Hamlets	Comm.Lnd	E.Lnd
St Giles/Fields	Middlesex	Ossulstone	St Giles	Holborn	Camden	Comm.Lnd	N.Mdx
St Katharine/T.[25]	Middlesex	Ossulstone	Whitechapel	Stepney	Tower Hamlets	St Kath.	E.Lnd
St Luke Old St.	Middlesex	Ossulstone	Holborn	Finsbury	Islington	St Paul's	N.Mdx
St Martin/Fields	Middlesex	Westminster	Strand	Westminster	Westminster	W'min/ Archd.Lnd	N.Mdx
St Mary Cray	Kent	Ruxley	Bromley	n/a	Bromley	Shore	NW.Kent
St Marylebone	Middlesex	Ossulstone	Marylebone	St Marylebone	Westminster	Comm.Lnd	N.Mdx
St Mary le Strand	Middlesex	Westminster	Strand	Westminster	Westminster	Archd.Mdx	N.Mdx
St Pancras[26]	Middlesex	Ossulstone	St Pancras	St Pancras	Camden	St Paul's	N.Mdx
St Paul's Cray	Kent	Ruxley	Bromley	Bromley	Bromley	Archd.Roc	NW.Kent
St Sepulchre	Middlesex	Ossulstone	Holborn[37]	Holborn	Camden	Comm.Lnd	N.Mdx
Sanderstead	Surrey	Wallington	Croydon	n/a	Croydon	Sry	E.Sry
Shadwell	Middlesex	Ossulstone	Stepney	Stepney	Tower Hamlets	Comm.Lnd	E.Lnd
Shepperton[1]	Middlesex	Spelthorne	Staines	n/a	n/a	Archd.Mdx	W.Mdx
Shoreditch	Middlesex	Ossulstone	Shoreditch	Shoreditch	Hackney	St Paul's	E.Lnd
Soho[28]	Middlesex	Westminster	Strand[29]	Westminster	Westminster	Archd.Mdx	N.Mdx
South Mimms	Middlesex	Edmonton[30]	Barnet	n/a	Barnet	Comm.Lnd	N.Mdx
Southwark							
Christ Church[31]	Surrey	Southwark	St Saviour	Southwark	Southwark	Sry/Lnd	E.Sry
St George[32]	Surrey	Southwark	St George S.	Southwark	Southwark	Sry/Lnd	E.Sry
St John[33]	Surrey	Southwark	St Olave	Bermondsey	Southwark	Sry/Lnd	E.Sry
St Olave	Surrey	Southwark	St Olave	Bermondsey	Southwark	Sry/Lnd	E.Sry
St Saviour[34]	Surrey	Southwark	St Saviour	Southwark	Southwark	Sry/Lnd	E.Sry
St Thomas	Surrey	Southwark	St Olave	Bermondsey	Southwark	Sry/Lnd	E.Sry
Spitalfields	Middlesex	Ossulstone	Whitechapel	Stepney	Tower Hamlets	Comm.Lnd	E.Lnd
Staines[1]	Middlesex	Spelthorne	Staines	n/a	n/a	Archd.Mdx	W.Mdx

Parish	County	Hundred	Reg. Dist.	Metro. Borough	London Borough	Probate	FHS
Stanwell[1]	Middlesex	Spelthorne	Staines	n/a	n/a	Archd.Mdx	W.Mdx
Stepney	Middlesex	Ossulstone	Stepney	Stepney	Tower Hamlets	Comm.Lnd	E.Lnd
Stoke Newington[35]	Middlesex	Ossulstone	Hackney	Stoke Newington	Hackney	St Paul's	E.Lnd
Stratford Bow[36]	Middlesex	Ossulstone	Poplar	Poplar	Tower Hamlets	Comm.Lnd	E.Lnd
Streatham	Surrey	Brixton	Wandsworth	Wandsworth	Lambeth	Sry/Lnd	E.Sry
Sunbury[1]	Middlesex	Spelthorne	Staines	n/a	n/a	Archd.Mdx	W.Mdx
Sutton	Surrey	Wallington	Epsom	n/a	Sutton	Sry	E.Sry
Teddington	Middlesex	Spelthorne	Kingston	n/a	Richmond	Comm.Lnd	W.Mdx
Tooting[37]	Surrey	Brixton	Wandsworth	Wandsworth	Wandsworth	Sry/Lnd	E.Sry
Tottenham	Middlesex	Edmonton	Edmonton	n/a	Haringey	Comm.Lnd	N.Mdx
Twickenham	Middlesex	Isleworth	Brentford	n/a	Richmond	Archd.Mdx	W.Mdx
Twyford[38]	Middlesex	Ossulstone	Brentford	n/a	Ealing	not known	W.Mdx
Upminster	Essex	Chafford	Romford	n/a	Havering	Archd.Ess	E.Lnd
Uxbridge[39]	Middlesex	Elthorne	Uxbridge	n/a	Hillingdon	Archd.Mdx	W.Mdx/Hill
Walthamstow	Essex	Becontree	West Ham	n/a	Waltham Forest	Comm.Lnd	Waltham
Wandsworth	Surrey	Brixton	Wandsworth	Wandsworth	Wandsworth	Sry/Lnd	E.Sry
Wanstead	Essex	Becontree	West Ham	n/a	Redbridge	Archd.Ess	E.Lnd
Wapping	Middlesex	Ossulstone	Stepney	Stepney	Tower Hamlets	Comm.Lnd	E.Lnd
Wennington	Essex	Chafford	Romford	n/a	Havering	Archd.Ess	E.Lnd
West Drayton	Middlesex	Elthorne	Uxbridge	n/a	Hillingdon	St Paul's	
W.Mdx/Hill							
West Ham	Essex	Becontree	West Ham	n/a	Newham	Archd.Ess	E.Lnd

Westminster

St Anne see Soho

St Clement see St Clement Danes

St George see St George Hanover Square

St James[40]	Middlesex	Westminster	Westminster	Westminster	Westminster	Archd.Mdx	N.Mdx
St John	Middlesex	Westminster	St George	Westminster	Westminster	W'min	N.Mdx
St Margaret	Middlesex	Westminster	St George	Westminster	Westminster	Archd.Mdx/ W'min	N.Mdx
St Martin see St Martin in the Fields						
St Mary see St Mary le Strand						
St Paul see Covent Garden						
West Twyford see Twyford						
West Wickham	Kent	Ruxley	Bromley	n/a	Bromley	Archd.Roc	NW.Kent
Whitechapel	Middlesex	Ossulstone	Whitechapel	Stepney	Tower Hamlets	Comm.Lnd	E.Lnd
Willesden	Middlesex	Ossulstone	Hendon	n/a	Brent	St Paul's	N.Mdx
Wimbledon	Surrey	Brixton	Kingston	n/a	Merton	Croydon	E.Sry
Woodford	Essex	Becontree	West Ham	n/a	Redbridge	Comm.Lnd	E.Lnd
Woolwich[41] Woolw.	Kent	Blackheath	Greenwich[42]	Woolwich	Greenwich	Archd.Roc	NW.Kent/

Notes to Appendix 2

1. These parishes were transferred to the administrative county of Surrey in 1965, but their records are generally at London Metropolitan Archives.
2. Until 1869. After 1869 in St Olave Registration District.
3. Old Brentford was in the parish of Ealing until 1828.
4. Also known as Bromley St Leonard.
5. There is a completely different Blackheath Hundred in Surrey. However, no part of it was incorporated in Greater London.
6. Most, but not all of this parish remained outside the Greater London area in 1965.
7. Part Blackheath Hundred, part Ruxley Hundred, entirely Ruxley Hundred by the nineteenth century.
8. The ancient parish of St Nicholas Deptford was mainly in Blackheath Hundred, Kent and in the diocese of Rochester. However, a part called Hatcham was in Brixton Hundred, Surrey. In 1730, a church was built in Hatcham known as St Paul Deptford.
9. Renamed Sidcup in 1925.
10. Sometimes known as Great Greenford, to distinguish from Perivale or Little Greenford.
11. Often known as East Greenwich.
12. Not to be confused with Hampstead Garden Suburb, a part of Hendon not created a parish until 1911.
13. After 1848. From 1837-48 part of Edmonton Registration District.
14. Often known as St Andrew Holborn, St Andrew, London or St Andrew, Middlesex
15. Not to be confused with Hornsey Rise, an area created a parish in 1865 out of part of Islington.
16. Sometimes known as Whitchurch.
17. New Malden is a separate though nearby area, created from Kingston parish.
18. This parish should not be confused with Stoke Newington in Middlesex. It is often found in records as Newington Butts
19. Until 1869. After 1869 in St Saviour Registration District.
20. In additon to the Middlesex parish, there is a part of the ancient county of Surrey called Norwood. Part of this area was in Lambeth and was made a separate parish in 1825. The other part was in Croydon, and became a separate parish in 1845.
21. Sometimes known as Little Greenford.
22. Until 1868. After 1868 in Woolwich Registration District.
23. Until 1869. After 1869 in St Olave Registration District.
24. Part Westminster, part Ossulstone Hundred.
25. St Katharine by the Tower was a Royal Peculiar. It was almost entirely converted into a dock in 1825.
26. Not to be confused with St Pancras Soper Lane, a small parish in the City of London.
27. After 1845. Until 1845 in West London Registration District.
28. Also known as St Anne, Westminster.

29. Until 1868, afterwards in Westminster Registration District.
30. Part in Cashio Hundred, Hertfordshire
31. Also known as Christ Church, Surrey.
32. Also known as St George, Surrey.
33. Also known as St John Horsleydown.
34. Also known as Southwark Cathedral, and in early records as St Mary Overy.
35. This parish should not be confused with Newington in Surrey, which is often found in records as Newington Butts.
36. Not to be confused with Stratford, Essex, which was not an ancient parish, and was created in 1844 from West Ham. The districts are not far from one another, but completely separate. Also not to be confused with the church of St Mary le Bow in the City of London, which is completely separate.
37. The parish was called Tooting Graveney or Lower Tooting. Tooting Bec or Upper Tooting was part of Streatham.
38. Also known as West Twyford or Twyford Abbey.
39. Technically, Uxbridge was merely a chapelry of Hillingdon until 1827, but it kept registers, was the principal centre of population, and in all ways was treated as parochial.
40. Also known as St James Piccadilly.
41. Part of this parish extended north of the Thames. It was incorporated with parts of East Ham into a parish called Victoria Docks St Mary in 1864. The Woolwich part was detached in 1877 to form St John the Evangelist, North Woolwich parish.
42. Until 1868. After 1868 in Woolwich Registration District.

APPENDIX 3
The suburbs and smaller areas of London

S ubstantial places which were not ancient parishes or which are of a unusual nature or status are listed below, keyed to their ancient parish or parishes where appropriate. References to 'early registers' means before 1837. No such list can pretend to be exhaustive, but most suburbs are listed.

Abbey Wood. A part of Plumstead.

Addiscombe. A part of Croydon until 1879.

Agar Town. A part of St Pancras until 1862.

Aldborough. Hatch Created from Great Ilford in 1863.

Aldersbrook. Created from Little Ilford and Wanstead in 1914.

Alperton. Originally a part of Harrow, it was then part of Wembley when that was separated from Harrow, and became a parish in 1904.

Angell Town. A part of Brixton in Lambeth until 1853.

Arnos Grove. An area in Edmonton.

Artillery Ground. Old A liberty outside the City walls, between St Botolph. Bishopsgate in the City and Spitalfields.

Balham. A part of Streatham until 1855.

Barkingside. A part of Great Ilford until 1841.

Barnard's Inn. An extra-parochial place and Inn of Chancery. It has no registers.

Barnsbury. A part of Islington until 1862.

Bayswater. A part of Paddington until 1858.

Becontree. A hundred in Essex, but with no parish church before 1922.

Bedford New Town. A part of St Pancras until 1859.

Bedford Park. Created from parts of Chiswick, Acton and Ealing in 1879.

Belgravia. An area in St George Hanover Square.

Bellingham. An area in Lewisham.

Belmont. Created from Cheam and Sutton in 1916.

Belsize Park. A part of Hampstead until 1861.

Belvedere. A part of Erith until 1861.

Benhilton. A part of Sutton until 1863.

Bensham. An area in Croydon.

Bexleyheath. A part of Bexley until 1866.

Bickley. A part of Bromley until 1866.

Blackfriars. A City of London parish is called St Anne Blackfriars. A bridge was built across the Thames from that parish, and an area on the south bank opposite the City parish became known as Blackfriars, from the Blackfriars Road which ran through it. This area was in the parish of Christ Church Southwark, which may sometimes be found named as such in census returns.

Blackheath. A part of Greenwich and Lewisham. In 1854 the Greenwich part was made parochial, in 1859 the Lewisham part.

Blackheath Park. A part of Charlton until 1886.

Blackwall. An area in Poplar.

Bounds Green. Created from parts of Edmonton and Tottenham in 1906.

Brent. A river which gave its name to Brentford and, latterly, a London Borough.

Bridewell Precinct. A precinct between St Bride and St Anne Blackfriars in the City. It had a chapel, with registers which are at the Guildhall Library.

Brixton. A part of Lambeth until 1825.

Brockley. A part of Lewisham until 1855.

Brompton. A part of Kensington until 1830. West Brompton was created in 1850.

Brondesbury. A part of Willesden until 1867.

Brownswood Park. A part of Hornsey until 1875.

Bunhill Fields. An area in Finsbury famous for its nonconformist burial ground.

Burnt Oak. An area in Edgware.

Bushey Park. An area in Hampton.

Cambridge Heath. An area in Bethnal Green.

Camden Town. Camden Chapel has some early registers, but not made a parish (out of St Pancras) until 1852. Camden was the name chosen for a London Borough in 1965, covering Hampstead, Holborn and St Pancras.

Campden Hill. A part of Kensington until 1865.

Canning Town. A part of West Ham and its daughter parishes in Plaistow until 1879.

Canonbury. A part of Islington.

Castlebar Hill. An area in Ealing.

Catford. A part of Lewisham until 1888.

Chadwell Heath. Created from Dagenham and Great Ilford in 1895.

Champion Hill. A part of East Dulwich in Camberwell until 1881.

Charing Cross. An area in St Martin in the Fields.

Charterhouse. An extra-parochial place between Clerkenwell and St Sepulchre, with a chapel whose early registers have been printed.

Chipping Barnet. A part of East Barnet until 1866.

Clapton. A part of Hackney until 1855.

Clifford's Inn. An extra-parochial place and Inn of Chancery. It has no registers.

Clink. A liberty in St Saviour Southwark.

Cockfosters. An area in Enfield.

Colindale. A part of Hendon until 1951.

Collier Row. A part of Romford until 1955.

Coombe. A part of Kingston, never made parochial on its own, but united with New Malden in 1867.

Cricklewood. A part of Hendon until 1892.

Crofton Park. A part of Lewisham until 1900.

Crouch End. An area in Hornsey.

Crystal Palace. A part of Penge (see below).

Cubitt Town. A part of Poplar until 1873.

Dalston. A part of Hackney until 1844.

DeBeauvoir. Town. A part of Hackney until 1842.

Denmark Hill. A part of Brixton in Lambeth until 1848.

Dollis Hill. Originally a part of Willesden, it was made a parish in 1939 from Neasden (q.v.).

Downe. A part of Orpington until 1861.

Downham. An area in Lewisham.

Dulwich. A part of Camberwell until 1865, but there are early registers of the College chapel there.

Earl's Court. An area of Kensington.

Earlsfield. A part of Wandsworth until 1890.

Eastcote. A part of Ruislip until 1931.

East Wickham. A part of Plumstead until 1854.

Elephant and Castle. An area in Newington (Surrey).

Ely Place. See Saffron Hill.

Finsbury. A borough, but not a parish until 1842 when created from St Luke Old Street. Not to be confused with the next entry which is completely separate,

Finsbury Park. A part of Islington until 1888. Not to be confused with the completely separate area noted in the previous entry.

Forest Gate. Created from East Ham and West Ham in 1852.

Forest Hill. A part of Camberwell and Lewisham until 1855.

Frognal. An area in Hampstead.

Furnival's Inn. An extra-parochial place and Inn of Chancery. It has no registers.

Gipsy Hill. A part of Norwood in Lambeth until 1867.

Glasshouse Yard. An extra-parochial liberty. It has no registers, its inhabitants using St Botolph Aldersgate in the City of London, but some civil parish records survive.

Golder's Green. A part of Hendon until 1914.

Goodmayes. Created from Barking, Great Ilford and Dagenham in 1914.

Gospel Oak. An area in St Pancras.

Gray's Inn. An extra-parochial place and Inn of Court. It has some registers of its chapel.

Grosvenor Park. A part of Walworth in Newington until 1871.

Grove Park. An area in Lewisham.

Gunnersbury. Created from Ealing, Chiswick and Acton in 1888.

Haggerston. A part of Shoreditch until 1830.

Halliford. An area in Shepperton.

Ham. A part of Kingston until 1834. Often found in early taxation lists separate from Kingston, entitled Ham and Hatch.

Hampton Wick. A part of Hampton until 1831.

Hanger Lane. This name can cause confusion. Originally there was a place called Hanger Hill in Ealing, and a place called Hanger Lane in Tottenham. The name Hanger Lane does not seem to still be used in Tottenham, probably to avoid confusion with the Ealing place, as when an underground railway station was built there in the twentieth century it was named Hanger Lane, not Hanger Hill, and that is how the area is now generally known.

Harlesden. Created from Acton, Hammersmith and Willesden in 1875.

Harold Wood. A part of Hornchurch until 1938.

Harringay. A 1965 London Borough, but spelled Haringey. It was created a parish in 1892 from Hornsey and Tottenham.

Hatcham. See Deptford in parish list.

Hatch End. A part of Pinner until 1906.

Hatton Garden. See Saffron Hill.

Havering-atte-Bower. A ward and liberty in Hornchurch, created a parish in 1836.

Haverstock Hill. A part of St Pancras until 1852.

Heathrow. An area in Hillingdon, now the main London airport.

Herne Hill. Created from Camberwell and Lambeth in 1845.

Highams Park. A part of Walthamstow until 1912.

Highbury. A part of Islington until 1849.

Highgate. A chapel with early registers, but was not parochial until 1834, when created from Hornsey and St Pancras.

Hither Green. An area in Lewisham.

Holloway. A part of Islington until 1830.

Holywell. An area in Shoreditch.

Homerton. A part of Hackney until 1846.

Hook. A hamlet in Kingston, made parochial in 1852. Sometimes appears separately in early taxation lists.

Horsleydown. See Southwark St John in parish list.

Hounslow. A town with a chapel with some early registers, but not parochial until 1836, when created from Heston and Isleworth.

Hoxton. A part of Shoreditch until 1830.

Hurlingham. An area in Fulham.

Inner Temple. See Temple below.

Isle of Dogs. An area of Poplar.

Kenley. An area in Coulsdon and Caterham, Surrey, made parochial in 1889.

Kennington. A part of Lambeth until 1825.

Kensal Green. Created from parts of Chelsea, Kensington, Hammersmith, Paddington and Willesden in 1845.

Kentish Town. Not in Kent - a chapel in St Pancras with some early registers. Was made parochial in 1863.

Ken Wood. An area in St Pancras.

Kidbrooke. A liberty in Blackheath Hundred, made into a parish in 1889.

Kilburn. An area in Hampstead.

King's Cross. An area in St Pancras.

Kingsland. An area in Shoreditch.

Knightsbridge. A chapelry of St Margaret Westminster with some early registers.

Ladywell. An area in Lewisham.

Lavender Hill. A part of Battersea until 1875.

Leigham Court. An area in Streatham.

Leytonstone. A part of Leyton until 1845.

Lincoln's Inn. An extra-parochial place and Inn of Court. It has some registers.

Lisson Grove. A part of St Marylebone until 1838.

Longford. An area in Harmondsworth.

Loughborough Park. A part of Brixton in Lambeth until 1877.

Lyonsdown. A part of East Barnet until 1869.

Lyon's Inn. An extra-parochial place and Inn of Chancery. It has no registers.

Maida Hill. Created from parts of Paddington and St Marylebone in 1876, includes the area later known as Maida Vale.

Mayfair. A part of St George Hanover Square until 1865, however with an early chapel with registers.

Middle Temple. See Temple below.

Mile End New Town. A hamlet in Stepney, in which various churches were built from the 1840s on.

Mile End Old Town. Also a hamlet in Stepney, in which various churches were built from the 1840s on.

Mill Hill. A part of Hendon until 1833.

Millwall. A part of Poplar until 1870.

Motspur Park. An area in Malden.

Mottingham. A part of Eltham until 1884.

Muswell Hill. A part of Hornsey until 1843.

Neasden. A part of Kingsbury and Willesden until 1885.

New Cross. An area in St Paul Deptford.

Noak Hill. An area in Romford.

Noel Park. A part of Wood Green in Tottenham until 1889.

Norbiton. A part of Kingston until 1842.

Norbury. A part of Croydon until 1907.

Northwood. Created from Ruislip in 1854, with the transfer of small parts of Rickmansworth and Watford in Hertfordshire.

Norton. Folgate An extra-parochial place bounded by Spitalfields, Shoreditch. St Botolph Bishopsgate (in the City) and the Old Artillery Ground. It has no registers, but some civil parish records survive.

Norwood Green. An area in Norwood.

Notting Hill. A part of Kensington until 1845.

Nunhead. A part of Peckham in Camberwell until 1878.

Old Artillery Ground. An extra-parochial place. It has no registers, but some civil parish records survive.

Old Ford. A part of Stratford le Bow until 1858.

Osterley Park. An area in Heston.

Palmer's Green. A part of Edmonton until 1906.

Paris Garden. A liberty in St Saviour Southwark, which was made into the parish of Christ Church Southwark in 1670.

Parsons Green. An area in Fulham.

Peckham. A part of Camberwell until 1842.

Pentonville. A chapelry in Clerkenwell, with some early registers, it was made parochial in 1862.

Penge. An outlying hamlet of Battersea. It was sufficiently far away that few if any inhabitants would have used Battersea church. A church was not built until 1851. In 1899 it was transferred to the administrative county of Kent, and in 1965 to the Greater London area as part of the London Borough of Bromley.

Perry Hill. A part of Lewisham until 1880.

Petts Wood. Created from Orpington and Chislehurst in 1935.

Piccadilly. See St James Westminster in parish list.

Pimlico. A part of St George Hanover Square until 1830.

Plaistow. A part of West Ham until 1844.

Ponders End. A part of Enfield until 1899.

Portland Town. A part of St Marylebone until 1849.

Portpool. A precinct including Gray's Inn.

Potter's Bar. A part of South Mimms until 1835.

Primrose Hill. A part of Hampstead until 1885.

Purley. Created from Coulsdon, Beddington, Sanderstead and Croydon in 1884.

Queen Square. Another name for St George the Martyr, Holborn, for which see main parish list.

Ratcliff or Ratcliffe. A hamlet partly in Stepney, partly in Limehouse, made a separate parish in 1840.

Ravensbury. An area in Morden.

Raynes Park. A part of Merton until 1907.

Regent's Park. A part of St Pancras until 1853.

Riddlesdown. A part of Coulsdon until 1925.

Roehampton. A part of Putney until 1845.

Rolls Liberty. A liberty close to St Dunstan in the West. From 1842 to 1886 there was a church in this Liberty and registers were kept, but it was then united to St Dunstan. Some civil parish records survive.

Roxeth. A part of Harrow until 1863.

Ruskin Park. An area of Brixton in Lambeth.

Sadler's Wells. An area in Clerkenwell.

Saffron Hill, Hatton Garden, Ely Rents and **Ely Place**. A liberty next to Holborn. The only early separate registers are of the bishop of Ely's chapel in his London home - Ely Place. A church which kept registers was built in 1839. Some civil parish records survive.

St Helier. Created from parts of Morden, Carshalton and Sutton in 1930.

St John's Wood. A part of St Marylebone until 1846.

St Margaret's. A part of Isleworth until 1898.

St Martin le Grand. A liberty later incorporated in St Leonard Foster Lane and St Ann and St Agnes Aldersgate. No separate registers exist.

Savoy. A liberty close to St Mary le Strand with a chapel with early registers.

Scotland Yard. A place in St Martin in the Fields.

Selhurst. An area in Croydon.

Selsdon. Created from parts of Croydon and Addington in 1934.

Serjeants' Inn. Two separate extra-parochial places (one in Fleet Street and one in Court Lane) and Inns of Chancery. They have no registers.

Seven Dials. An area in St Giles in the Fields.

Seven Sisters. An area in Tottenham.

Shacklewell. A part of Hackney until 1929.

Sheen. East Sheen was Mortlake, Sheen or West Sheen was Richmond.

Shepherd's Bush. A part of Hammersmith until 1883.

Shirley. A part of Croydon until 1846.

Sidcup. Foots Cray, Kent was renamed Sidcup in 1925. See parish list.

Silvertown. An area of East Ham.

Slade Green. Created from Crayford and Erith in 1925.

Smithfield. There are two Smithfields. East Smithfield is the part of St Botolph Aldgate outside the City. West Smithfield is an area (historically containing the meat market) in the City parish of St Bartholomew the Less.

Somers Town. A part of St Pancras until 1852. Not to be confused with Summers Town (q.v.).

Southall. A part of Norwood until 1850, but with registers from a few years earlier.

Southfields. Created from Wandsworth and Wimbledon in 1922.

Southgate. A chapelry in Edmonton, with early registers and created a parish in 1851.

Spring Grove. Created from Heston, Hounslow and Isleworth in 1856.

Squirrel's Heath. Created from Romford and Hornchurch in 1926.

Stamford Bridge. An area in Fulham.

Stamford Brook. A part of Hammersmith until 1888. Not to be confused with the next entry.

Stamford Hill. A part of Hackney until 1828. Not to be confused with the previous entry.

Staple Inn. An extra-parochial place and Inn of Chancery. It has no registers.

Stockwell. A part of Lambeth until 1845.

Stonebridge. A part of Willesden until 1892.

Stroud Green. A part of Hornsey until 1881.

Sudbury. A part of Harrow and its daughter parishes until 1923.

Summerstown. A part of Wandsworth until 1845. Not to be confused with Somers Town (q.v.).

Surbiton. A part of Kingston until 1845.

Sydenham. A part of Lewisham until 1855.

Telford Park. A part of Streatham until 1903.

Temple. The An extra-parochial place with two Inns of Court, the Inner Temple and the Middle Temple. The Temple church has early registers which have been printed.

Thavies Inn. An extra-parochial place and Inn of Chancery. It has no registers.

Thornton Heath. A part of Croydon until 1871.

Tollington Park. A part of Islington until 1854.

Tolworth. A detached part of the parish of Long Ditton, Surrey. There was no separate church at Tolworth until 1895. It was incorporated in the London Borough of Kingston in 1965, unlike the rest of Long Ditton, which remained in Surrey.

Tothill Fields. Created from St John Westminster in 1841.

Totteridge. Chapelry in Bishop's Hatfield, Broadwater Hundred, Hertfordshire until 1892. Later incorporated in London Borough of Barnet.

Tower of London. An extra-parochial place with a chapel. It has early registers.

Tower Without. Old. An extra-parochial place, next to the Tower of London. It has no registers.

Tufnell Park. A part of Islington until 1868.

Tulse Hill. Created from Brixton and Norwood in Lambeth, and Streatham in 1856.

Turnham Green. A part of Chiswick until 1845.

Tyburn. The old name for St Marylebone.

Upton Park. Created from East Ham and West Ham in 1887.

Vauxhall. A part of Lambeth until 1861.

Victoria Docks. A part of East Ham until 1864.

Waddon. An area in Croydon.

Walham Green. A part of Fulham until 1835.

Wallington. This is the name of a Surrey hundred, but there is no ancient parish church, the church there only being built in 1867. However, Wallington was always treated as a separate civil parish from Beddington with which it was united for ecclesiastical purposes.

Walworth. A part of Newington until 1825.

Wealdstone. Created from parts of Harrow and Pinner in 1882.

Wembley. A part of Harrow until 1847.

Westbourne Park. Created from Kensington and Paddington in 1871.

Westcombe Park. A part of Greenwich until 1892.

Whetstone. A part of Finchley until 1833.

Whitehall Park. Created from parts of Hornsey and Islington in 1897. Not to be confused with the street called Whitehall in central London.

Whitchurch. Another name for Little Stanmore see parish list.

Whitefriars. Precinct between the Temple and St Bride in the City. Its inhabitants used the latter church.

Whitton. A part of Twickenham until 1862.

Winchmore Hill. A part of Edmonton until 1851.

Wood Green. A chapelry in Tottenham, created a parish in 1866.

Wormwood Scrubs. An area in Hammersmith.

Yeading. An area in Hayes.

Yiewsley. A chapelry in Hillingdon, created a parish in 1874.

APPENDIX 4
Addresses of London family history society secretaries

East of London Family History Society
New Membership Secretary: 37 Medora Road, Romford RM7 7EP.
Email: chairman@eolfhs.org.uk ◆ Website: www.eolfhs.org.uk/eolintro.htm

East Surrey Family History Society
Cobham Close, South Wallington, Surrey, SM6 9DS.
Email: secretary@eastsurreyfhs.org.uk ◆ Website: www.eastsurreyfhs.org.uk/

Hillingdon Family History Society
Mrs G. May, 20 Moreland Drive, Gerrards Cross, Bucks SL9 8BB.
Email: Gillmay@dial.pipex.com ◆ Website: www.rootsweb.com/~enghfhs/

London Westminster and North Middlesex Family History Society
Mrs Joan I. Pyemont, 57 Belvedere Way, Kenton, Harrow HA3 9XQ.
Email: william.pyemont@virgin.net ◆ Website: www.lnmfhs.dircon.co.uk/

Waltham Forest Family History Society
Mr B.F. Burton, 49 Sky Peals Road, Woodford Green, Essex IG8 9NE.

West Middlesex Family History Society
Mr Tony Simpson, 32 The Avenue, Bedford Park, Chiswick, W4 1HT.
Website: www.west-middlesex-fhs.org.uk

West Surrey Family History Society
Email: secretary@wsfhs.org ◆ Website: www.wsfhs.org/

Woolwich and District Family History Society
Mrs E. Reynolds, 54 Parkhill Road, Bexley, Kent DA5 1HY
Email: FrEdnaFHS@aol.com

APPENDIX 5

Online resources for London and Middlesex censuses

This table (overleaf) shows the main commercial sites which offer online census indexes, etc. to London. Their fees vary, and only the researcher can determine which, if any, to join, having regard of course to their other material. For example, Ancestry.com clearly has the most census material, but is much weaker pre-1837 than Origins. The author also has serious questions about its accuracy as compared with Origins. Where possible, e.g. in the Society of Genealogists' own library, both sites should be searched.

1881 has been omitted because it is freely available (FamilySearch.org). Fairly small parts of some London censuses (especially the 1891) are freely available on the FreeCen site (freepages.genealogy.rootsweb.com/).

Most of the transcription was done abroad. The exception is The Genealogist, where much of the transcription and indexing was done by volunteers. A crosscheck showed, perhaps surprisingly, that there were more errors in this work than that done by paid assistance, however this is likely to be very variable. The Genealogist also has more limited coverage, outer Middlesex not being covered for some of the census years.

Year		1841	1851	1861	1871	1891	1901	1911
Ancestry.Com	Index	Yes	Yes	Yes	Yes	Yes	Yes	No
	Transcript	Yes	Yes	Yes	Yes	Yes	Yes	No
	Image	Yes	Yes	Yes	Yes	Yes	Yes	No
Origins	Index	Yes	No	Yes	Yes	No	No	No
	Transcript	Yes	No	Yes	Yes	No	No	No
	Image	Yes	No	Yes	Yes	No	No	No
The Genealogist	Index	Yes	Yes	Yes	Yes	Yes	Yes	No
	Transcript	No	Yes	Yes	Yes	No	No	No
	Image	No	Yes	Yes	Yes	No	No	No
Findmypast	Index	Yes	No	Yes	Yes	No	No	Yes
	Transcript	Yes	No	Yes	Yes	No	No	Yes
	Image	Yes	No	Yes	Yes	No	No	Yes
Stepping Stones	Index	No	No	No	No	No	No	No
	Transcript	No	No	No	No	No	No	No
	Image	Yes	Yes	Yes	Yes	Yes	Yes	No

CITY OF LONDON AND METROPOLITAN BOROUGHS 1900-1965

CITY OF LONDON AND LONDON BOROUGHS 1965-

About the SOCIETY OF GENEALOGISTS

Founded in 1911 the Society of Genealogists (SoG) is Britain's premier family history organisation. The Society maintains a splendid genealogical library and education centre in Clerkenwell.

The Society's collections are particularly valuable for research before the start of civil registration of births marriages and deaths in 1837 but there is plenty for the beginner too. Anyone starting their family history can book free help sessions in the open community access area where assistance can be given in searching online census indexes or looking for entries in birth, death and marriage indexes.

The Library contains Britain's largest collection of parish register copies, indexes and transcripts and many nonconformist registers. Most cover the period from the sixteenth century to 1837. Along with registers, the library holds local histories, copies of churchyard gravestone inscriptions, poll books, trade directories, census indexes and a wealth of information about the parishes where our ancestors lived.

Unique indexes include Boyd's Marriage Index with more than 7 million names compiled from 4300 churches between 1538-1837 and the Bernau Index with references to 4.5 million names in Chancery and other court proceedings. Also available are indexes of wills and marriage licences, and of apprentices and masters (1710-1774). Over the years the Society has rescued and made available records discarded by government departments and institutions but of great interest to family historians. These include records from the Bank of England, Trinity House and information on Teachers and Civil Servants.

Boyd's and other unique databases are published on line on **www.origins.com**, on **www.findmypast.com** and on the Society's own website **www.sog.org.uk**. There is free access to these and many other genealogical sites within the Library's Internet suite.

The Society is the ideal place to discover if a family history has already been researched with its huge collection of unique manuscript notes, extensive collections of past research and printed and unpublished family histories. If you expect to be carrying out family history research in the British Isles then membership is very worthwhile although non-members can use the library for a small search fee.

The Society of Genealogists is an educational charity. It holds study days, lectures, tutorials and evening classes and speakers from the Society regularly speak to groups around the country. The SoG runs workshops demonstrating computer programs of use to family historians. A diary of events and booking forms are available from the Society on 020 7553 3290 or on the website **www.sog.org.uk** .

Members enjoy free access to the Library, certain borrowing rights, free copies of the quarterly *Genealogists Magazine* and various discounts of publications, courses, postal searches along with free access to data on the members' area of our website and each quarter to our data on **www.origins.com**.

More details about the Society can be found on its extensive website at **www.sog.org.uk**

For a free Membership Pack contact the Society at:

14 Charterhouse Buildings,
Goswell Road,
London EC1M 7BA
Telephone 020 7553 3291
Fax 020 7250 1800

The Society is always happy to help with enquiries and the following contacts may be of assistance.

Library & shop hours:

Monday	Closed
Tuesday	10am - 6pm
Wednesday	10am - 6pm
Thursday	10am - 8pm
Friday	Closed
Saturday	10am - 6pm
Sunday	Closed

Contacts:

Membership
Tel: 020 7553 3291
Email: membership@sog.org.uk

Lectures & courses
Tel: 020 7553 3290
Email: events@sog.org.uk

Family history advice line
Tel: 020 7490 8911
See website for availability

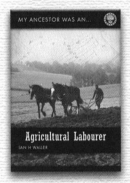